Your Historical Loveliness Knows No Bounds

Your Historical Loveliness Knows No Bounds

Form, Futurity, and Documentary Desire

WENDY XU

University of Michigan Press
Ann Arbor

Published in the United States of America by the
University of Michigan Press
First published October 2025

A CIP catalog record for this book is available from the British Library.

Library of Congress Cataloging-in-Publication data has been applied for.

ISBN: 978-0-472-04000-1 (paper : alk. paper)
ISBN: 978-0-472-22231-5 (ebook)

DOI: https://doi.org/10.3998/mpub.14487670

Cover image credit: Paris Musées / Musée Bourdelle

Authorized Representative: Easy Access System Europe, Mustamäe tee 50, 10621
Tallinn, Estonia, gpsr.requests@easproject.com

Contents

Digital materials related to this title can be found on the Fulcrum platform via the following citable URL: https://doi.org/10.3998/mpub.14487670

Figures

Acknowledgments

Grateful acknowledgment is given to the editors of the following publications where some of these writings first appeared, often in slightly different or excerpted form. Thank you for giving me the space to do my always imperfect thinking in public, and, in many cases, for your generous help in improving and deepening that thinking before publication.

"Reading Wang Wei in a Pandemic" —*Jewish Currents*
"What Is the Present For?" —*McSweeney's*
"Mignon, or, Further Notes on the Past" —*The Poetry Project Newsletter*
"Wendy Xu and Emily Lee Luan on Return, Form, and Longing" —*BOMB*
From "Notes for an Opening" —*Boston Review*, *Literary Hub*, *Triple Canopy*

These writings are a partial archive of my thinking around critical and creative ideas that have obsessed me for a very long time, which I've engaged both alone and with others, but most especially with my brilliant students at The New School since 2017, and at the Iowa Writers' Workshop in 2024, whose radical creativity and imagination continue to inspire. Thank you for helping to sharpen my thinking daily, and for allowing me to try and do the same for you. This book is deeply indebted to your vision and fierce intellectual magic.

Thanks also to the Iowa Writers' Workshop and Saltonstall Foundation for the Arts for support in order to work on this book in 2023–2024.

This text does not wish to be an overview or primer, not an intro to, even less a final word, a compendium, or a comprehensive guide to. Not for love of craft proclamations, and without instructive intent, I offer readings, inquiries, wormholes of memory, appreciations, and discontents instead, a tour of some of my most lively experiences as a reader of documentary texts and other projects of wild formal excitement. These writings are dedicated to the future.

Part One

Reading Wang Wei in a Pandemic

Recently, I've sought comfort in things that have been with me for a long time. I wear old clothing. I cook recipes from my childhood. And I keep circling back to the same long-loved poems.

Of all of these, "9/9, Thinking of My Brothers East of the Mountains," by the legendary Tang Dynasty poet Wang Wei, has been with me the longest, since before I was even born. It first found both of my parents in a grade-school classroom in Shandong, China—the "east of the mountains" referenced in the title—where, for a time, they were young classmates (I'm obsessed with this fact of their love story), and where they memorized the poem. Back then, it hadn't yet been translated into English with such great care and attention by David Hinton, whose version is the most crystalline and beautiful one I've come across:

9/9, THINKING OF MY BROTHERS EAST OF THE MOUNTAINS

Each year on this auspicious day, alone and foreign
here in a foreign place, my thoughts of you sharpen:

far away, I can almost see you reaching the summit,
dogwood berries woven into sashes, short one person.[1]

After we moved to the United States in 1989, perhaps feeling lonelier and more foreign than ever, heartsick for the Shandong of their and my birth, my parents would, on occasion, recite the poem to me in the original Chinese. Much later in life, I would come across it—independently for the first time—on the day of my thirtieth anniversary in this country. The poem has perhaps always been auspicious for me.

Away from home during Chongyang Festival (the ninth day of the ninth lunar month in the title), the poem's speaker reflects on another missed opportunity for gathering with loved ones by elegizing time itself. "Each year," they are alone and foreign. The recurrence of this sorrow is an unwanted anniversary.

But in its potency, the traveler's loneliness is also the source of the irrepressible vision in the poem's second half. The space taken up by the speaker's absence—both in the grammar of the line and in the imagined scene on the summit—always makes me cry. This poem is my favorite example of remembrance as astral projection, as teleportation, overcoming distance. The speaker's naming of their own absence transports them there into the image for us, the readers. It's a bittersweet kind of reunion that poetry grants, one that is beholden to, as the poem says, an "almost." Even the fantasy must reckon with the "almost," the asymptote of longing.

For much of my life I've felt shades of "alone and foreign / here in a foreign place," and current conditions have complicated the emotional implications of both "alone" and "foreign." Perhaps I have never felt *less* foreign to myself. Though, to others, at this moment: never more. I have been the homesick traveler of Wang Wei's poem as much as I have been the one holding space, unfailingly, for her return to the world.[2]

Writing Home

On Diasporic Language, Immigration, and Documentary Praxis

I begin in somewhat-obsession, with the idea of "writing home" and its valences, varied and rich. To write home is at once as simple and literal as it sounds, the act of writing to one who waits for you at home, the act carrying all the sweetness of that waiting and receiving. It's also one of the central challenges of representation for many immigrant or diasporic artists—we could say that to write, and to manifest (and for whom? more on that later) "home" on the page involves a collision of the imagined and the remembered, and desires for faithful representation give way to fantasizes of remaking the past to better serve the needs of the present. Whose needs? That too.

Equally challenging is the fact that to leave home via immigration or displacement or escape-as-necessity is an experience with clear beginning and no end, and is in this way more like a single point on a line extending infinitely in both directions (a double-headed arrow pointing toward the pre- and the post-), rather than the tidy distance between two fixed points. For myself and my own work, which is not the point of this writing but anecdotally related, this single point in time of my immigration and my Leaving Behind happens to occur three days before the events of June 4, 1989, in Tiananmen Square in Beijing, where the Chinese government violently cracked down on an enormous pro-democracy movement, and where the subsequent media coverage in the West produced the iconic "Unnamed Tank Man Protestor"[1] images that have by now lived a long life of their own, often used as visual shorthand for "resistance," political inspiration-porn, mapped onto any suitable struggle involving one-against-many.

I've never known how to talk *about* immigration in my work as a poet, the leaving and the not-crying (I was a baby after all, I didn't know), the rupture that my parents bore on my behalf. But I've tried, and I've often felt a melancholy in speaking directly to immigration's narrative or its lingering effects, a dissatisfaction as both artist and immigrant. Poetry allows a space to speak *through*—to bind immigration's effects (and thus affects) to the language of the poem itself, rather than to make immigration the subject of description, depiction. Immigration as point of view, attitude, dialect even, through which the poem speaks on whatever it wishes, an autographical (as opposed to auto-bio-graphical) opportunity for the self in flux.

Here I've borrowed an idea from Peter Gizzi, who suggests that "autography" is closer to what the poet does than autobiography,[2] the difference being that auto-bio-graphy means something like "the writing of the life of the self," subtly implying that both the life and the self are already lived, and finished, ready to be recorded and documented, while auto-grapy (as in autograph) links the act of writing with the self inextricably—so that writing conjures the self into being in real time, and thus for the self marked by immigration this idea has always helped me to further understand "writing home" as an act of genesis.

Conceptual ideas that orbit immigration—endlessness, flux, disembodiment—play upon the work as formal characteristics, and modify the textual body of the poem, enacting their effects upon grammatical and syntactical structures. Endlessness may feel in poem-time as linguistic restlessness, a delay in grammatical closure, an aggressive disruption of typical sentence patterning. Language itself is put under duress, in many cases by the gaze of the reader (mimicking hypervisibility, surveillance, and the like), and the fragmentation in response performs disembodiment and rootlessness as (again) grammatical gestures.

In my book *Phrasis* (2017),[3] which borrows its title from the second half of the tradition of ek-phrasis, no jade-hued waters or stinky-lunchbox poems appear. I'm drawn to ekphrasis as a tradition fundamentally aware of its own impossibility, in seeking to render in language visual art, which by its definition has no inherent need for it (language). But the ekphrastic writer, in a gesture of equally moving desire and arrogance, proceeds. The asymptote of ekphrastic desire mirrors the experience of writing "home" as an immigrant poet: The poem may infinitely approach home as an idea, and may retool itself infinite times and speak infinite tries, but may never arrive. Memory, much like the visual subjects of traditional ekphrasis, has no need for language, even snubs it, and speaks in sensation, image, bursts, and flutters.

So to write ekphrasis as a means of recovering an idealized lost home is a task steeped in both optimism and deep melancholy. In *Phrasis*, I decline the tradition of speaking toward/with/of fine art, and instead turns toward what I consider to be the more compelling visual rhetoric of our moment: the pervasive and sensationalized mass media imagery on television and screens that oversaturate our daily experience without any language at all, though *speak* they surely do.

Ekphrasis as both form (loosely) and methodology offers my work a point of entry into what begins amorphously as feeling, be it political or personal. And as text composed in my second language, *Phrasis* proposes that a diasporic language is something much more than the language of a diaspora spoken away from its place of origin. As a descriptor, "diasporic" points toward the grammatical flexibility and innovation required of the English language in order to function as secondary home, one for the immigrant mind rather than body. The language must also foreground the psychic challenges of immigration using improvisation, glitch, spontaneous performativity. The tension between speech, vision, narrative, and closure emerges freely.

From an ekphrastic period, I move toward documentary praxis. Among many useful definitions of "documentary poetry," none of which conflict, I always return to Philip Metres's supremely generous and succinct one that says "such poetry arises from the idea that poetry is not a museum-object to be observed from afar, but a dynamic medium that informs and is informed by the history of the moment."[4] This poetry aspires to more than being an object for aesthetic appreciation. It often holds at its core a concern for social justice or the centering of historically marginalized narratives, and it values intertextuality. When I ask my students who have never read "documentary poetry" what they think it will do, they easily provide the precise verbs. "Uncover." "Re-center." "Illuminate." Much like the figure of the immigrant in America who frustrates clean boundaries of identity and definition (and I would argue "usefulness"), documentary poetry with its hallmark formal hybridity questions traditional views about what is or isn't poetry, what it should or can look like.

But all this is not to imply that documentary poetry (docupoetry) does not have conventions, techniques, methods, lineages. One is the use of sourced language or language external to the poet, often from state-sanctioned official or bureaucratic spaces, typically foregrounding source and process. If the immigrant poet lives with the psychic simultaneity of both resisting and desiring assimilation, with varying degrees of shame and discomfort, does it align with docupoetry easily? If sourced language stands in for a "primary" language and experience, then the immigrant poet's technique of passing through and around this language, splicing and transgressing it, in many ways literalizes the lived experience of "secondary-ness." It is against forgetting that the poem moves.

I conceive of memory as a legitimate primary source text for docupoetry, and expand the designation beyond semantics. Though all writers draw on memory (and this is not, I don't think, controversial?) the complications of finding corroborating *documentation* for what is remembered makes this relationship particularly fraught for ESL, immigrant, undocumented, refugee, or otherwise displaced writers. When you add to this the unreliability of memory and the tendency to mythologize one's past over time, there naturally begins to manifest a disturbance in the language of the poem. The feeling of responsibility "to remember" sends the immigrant poet-documentarian toward archival spaces where an incomplete or more likely censored history is often waiting. The valence of *wanted* documentation, and the privileges denied when one does not exist in official capacity to the state, weigh heavily on the genre. A docupoetry methodology centers (rather than working to dissolve) this tension between the hyper-personal uncorroborated source text of memory, and the overly documented and surveilled realities of (in my case) American life, both wanted and unwanted, especially in the digital age. The gaps and slippages between the vying narratives of self that memory and reality offer are rich rather than reductive spaces for poetry.

Just one of many moving and illustrative examples of the field between memory and reality, and the efficacy of documentary praxis, is Don Mee Choi's 2016 collection *Hardly War*, a multilingual documentary work of poetry that is quite indescribable, but warrants the effort. Kaleidoscopic, formally dazzling, visual, and a meditation on war and America's brutal legacy in East and Southeast Asia (and beyond), *Hardly War* uses the author's father's photographs from the Vietnam War and Korean

War as a primary source text, and in doing so becomes just as personal as it is political.

Beneath a photograph taken by Choi's father of two refugee girls standing in front of a stalled M16 tank, an untitled poem by Choi is presented entirely in Korean hangul characters and ends with the following lines of English:

> I refuse to translate
> I refuse to translate
> I refuse to translate
> I refuse to translate
> I refuse to translate[5]

I read this as both statement of feeling and statement of craft, together forming something wilder and more nuanced than an ethos of refusal, though it is that as well. As feeling, it speaks first to the experience of the immigrant-foreigner as inundated (so as to warrant five refusals) with both explicit and implicit requests for accommodation and linguistic assistance by non-Korean-reading readers—Choi's repetitious refusal is ferocious in its stonewalling and in its unimpeachable No-ness, in response to a readership that would happily consume any salacious retelling of Foreigners Suffering.

As craft statement it similarly shows Choi at her most aware of audience, and gestures toward the author's technical disinterest as elsewhere in the project in contextualizing particular references, identity markers, or otherwise translating either literal Korean characters or cultural symbology. Choi untethers the value of speech-ing/writing from its ability to fulfill imperialist fantasies of good immigrants, characterized primarily by their legibility on the page and willingness to include *everybody*. This exact refusal and unwillingness to translate is or should be another central characteristic of "diasporic" language. The utopian desire that characterizes this language extends not only "backward" in hopes of reaching what has been lost, but forward toward a fantasy of speech where accommodation of a white Western or monolingual audience is not a prerequisite for access to social and political viability, not just *vis*ability. To refuse to translate is to mean "I refuse to be translatable *to* you" as well as "I refuse to translate *for* you" as a labor issue. This may manifest in a genre-agnostic approach to form, routinely both employing and disrespecting the genre conventions of poetry, memoir, and essay, due to underlying skepticism about the inherent value of their authority. Thus what we would not be wrong to call "hybrid-genre" work or "cross-genre" work is just as easily characterized as genre-*refusing* work, which for me better highlights the important sentiment of resentment, accommodation fatigue, and translation fatigue.

In contemporary poetry there is no shortage of poets working in this mode. Robyn Coste Lewis,[6] Srikanth Reddy,[7] Layli Long Soldier,[8] Myung Mi Kim,[9] Solmaz Sharif,[10] C. D. Wright,[11] and others come to mind, all of whom take up translation and legibility as central issues and who practice a kind of documentarian alchemy (using sourced and original language) in order to forge not just the auto-graphical self but the self in relation to unspeakable realities, nonetheless spoken of.

The Past (2021) humbly yet excitedly converses with these documentary poets. It is also a contribution to the small but significant canon of Tiananmen Square literature by authors like Liu Xiaobo,[12] Liu Xia,[13] Bei Dao,[14] and others—it offers the point of view of the secondhand or even "thirdhand" Tiananmen Square survivor, which I understand to be the Chinese immigrant held in diaspora by the same political forces that came down on the '89 generation, but who is shaped by '89 as primarily a psychological, not physical, threat. The psychic horrors of '89 have reverberating effects that cultivate obedience, fear, desire for assimilation as safety, and subservience, permanently marking a generation that came of age in Western countries in the shadow of such an ideology-destroying event. For an entire generation of Chinese immigrants, '89 wrote the rulebook for how to behave in order to survive a government, a question distressingly evergreen.

In situating '89 in my work as a second monumental "point" on the timeline, appearing three days after the moment of immigration-as-rupture, and by sourcing from both firsthand and scholarly materials on '89, I populate Tiananmen Square's "aftermath" with mutating/mutilating forms and the dissonant voices that (outside the world of the poem) are separated by history and thus cannot speak to one another.

Here I turn to Carolyn Forché's "Reading the Living Archives: The Witness of Literary Art" on the poetry of witness, who helpfully addresses the distinction between "after" and the word I'm choosing to use, "aftermath." Forché gives us that "aftermath" is not really (or only) a literal period of time, but

> a temporal debris field, where historical remains are strewn (of large events as well as those peripheral or lost) where "that which happened" remains present, including the consciousness in which such events arose.[15]

Forché does not privilege the reverberations resulting from traumatic events that can be remembered over those that are "peripheral or lost," setting them all equal in the space of "aftermath." This doubles as an elegant alternative phrasing of the "endlessness" of immigration, and it highlights the residue that remains (the slime trail or the breadcrumb trail, depending which you prefer) to disturb a language even in the absence of a direct retelling of one's immigration narrative. Though I am being careful not to represent immigration as solely a violence, it undoubtedly leaves its traces on the textual body.

Whether or not it's possible to "write home" in all these ways is secondary to what appears on the documentary poet's page, which is perhaps closer to a record of that process of trying, as opposed to a fulfillment of a fantasy of return. It is a suspended auto-graphical exercise against forgetting, and the desire of it moves rather indiscriminately between wanting to elegize the past and wanting to resurrect it. And even though these seem at odds, the effort does not feel Sisyphean to me, and the poem certainly does not experience it as punishment, rather as both a formal and an emotional energy that does not dissipate, but renews itself with each further word.

Documentary Traces, Relatability, and the Limits of Witness

That most nettlesome question, almost diabolical in its need and urgency: Who will think of me when I'm gone? What traces and smears, slime trails both wanted and unwanted will I leave behind to inspire any such thinking? This question should, it seems, in our surveilled and documented age, keep us up at night. Not only because we want to be loved, are loved, and remembered, but because daily and unwittingly we produce our unintentional yet deathless documents of our brief time on earth.

Ocean Vuong's "Amazon History of a Former Nail Salon Worker"[1] is what it declares itself to be—a chronological Amazon shopping history of an unnamed former nail salon worker whose purchases move from workplace supplies (nail polish colors, customer thank you cards) to remedies for a body increasingly battling pain (ibuprofen, heating packs) to finally the objects for facing terminal cancer (Chemo-Glam scarf, urn). It is a surreal and tender elegy, testifying to the painful process of both surviving and surviving *for* our most loved ones, in this case a mother survived by her son. The Amazon history itself is that most incidental, unintentional document that purports to exist to solve a problem Amazon has manufactured for its customers: not having an enumerated list of every item ever purchased from Amazon, with a quick link to reorder. In Vuong's poem, this history becomes an accidental inventory of the body's growing needs as it begins to fail, constituting a real-time memorial to a dying mother through the lens of her (diminishing) purchasing power as a consumer. She is an unnamed worker, but nonetheless first defined (by Amazon) by her worker status and first *recorded* as a series of transactions for work supplies. Though the poem begins in March, with the body already in need of pain relief ("Advil ibuprofen, 4 pack") It consists largely of the objects a nail salon worker may need to continue that work:

Mar.
Advil ibuprofen, 4 pack
Sally Hansen Pink Nail Polish, 6 pack
Clorox Bleach, industrial size
DIANE Hair pins, 4 pack
Small, handheld mirror
I Love New York T-shirt, white, small

Apr.
NongShim Ramen Noodle Bowl, 24 pack
Cotton Balls, 100 count
"Thank You For Your Loyalty" cards, 10 count
Toulene POR-15 40404 Solvent—1 Quart
UV LED Nail Lamp
Cuticle Oil, value pack
Clear Acrylic Nail Tips, 500 count[2]

Time continues to be marked neatly and chronologically in this monthly way, another Amazon convenience, including several months where purchases are not made. Instead, the month's blankness is held open with white space, requesting time and silence. To Amazon, this nail salon worker ostensibly does not exist for those months. To us, uncomfortably, she similarly does not, lost somewhere in the unyielding whiteness of the page. When purchasing resumes, time is again startlingly marked by the body's needs, its consumption of pain relief in growing quantifiable amounts, from regular strength ibuprofen to December's "Advil (ibuprofen) Maximum Strength, 4 pack."[3] The names of months persist, and go by, unaffected by pain or its attendant relief products.

What kind of inventory is this? Certainly one of work, of the toll on the body taken by customer service, the hell of "work ethic" perhaps (that immigrant requirement), of optimism, of the unseen supplies needed for participating in a workforce that anonymizes both your body and your pain. It is also of course an inventory of the size and strength of a mother's love, a mother's preparations for becoming an absence soon to her son:

Apr.
Chemo-Glam cotton scarf, Flower garden print
"Warrior Mom" Breast Cancer awareness T-shirt, Pink and White

May.
Mueller 255 Lumbar Support Back Brace

Jun.
Birthday Card—Son—We Will Always Be Together, *Snoopy* design[4]

As the body's pain grows increasingly untamable, urgent and needy of relief, it's the language of packaging and *product* inventory that ironically provides our only units of measurement for understanding the subject's suffering. From four packages of ibuprofen per season to four packages per month—this document is one of need, and the insatiable demands of pain atop which a company like Amazon stacks its endless profits. One should also think here of the Amazon worker themselves, the picker fulfilling an order in the cavernous warehouse whose body, in a convenience economy, endures pain in order to ship pain relief to another worker. The optimism and despair of each purchase is written out on the body of these two workers in dialectical interdependence. We might imagine that on a day off, the Amazon picker too might stop by a nail salon for some relief and respite.

The language of Vuong's poem clangs and roars in the ear technical, branded, and unfeeling. If there's lyricism here it's corrupt and uncanny, a hollow approximation of both cheer and care found in items like "NewChic Ochre Summer Dress Floral Print, Sz 6," "CozyNites Fleece Blanket, pink," and products simply branded "Chemo-Glam."[5] The tenderness and sorrow of Vuong's poem comes through not *despite* its external "unemotive" language, and the lack of the lyric pronoun, but because of it. Some memorials (and memories too) are made by accident, were even unwanted in one's lifetime. Horribly and reliably, who keeps your memory going up until death? Amazon does. Who makes sure you see all of the products you need? Amazon. Who is remembering you after you're gone? Certainly not Amazon if your purchasing habits cease, but potentially the eventual wearer of "wool socks, grey, 1 pair,"[6] the last item on this Amazon shopper's list. This record's quiet violence is also the memorialization of one anonymous worker's participation in another worker's abstraction, their dependency spanning distances and months and years. In a convenience economy, Amazon assures us that at least we won't face our own deaths unprepared.

Toward the poem's end, the body's needs grow slim, at least its needs for which Amazon carries a remedying product. In July, a purchase for the future:

> *Jul.*
> Beautiful Life Urn, Dove and Rose engraved, small Perfect Memories
> picture frame, 8x11 in, black
> Burt's Bees chap stick, Honey, 1 pcs

And in August, nothing, though in October:

> *Oct.*
> YourStory Customized Memorial Plaque, 10x4x8in.
> Winter coat, navy blue, x-small[7]

Who is making these purchases, heavy in their finality and purpose? It may be the mother or her son. It may be a purchase made together, in preparation for the inevitable. Just as the reader doesn't know, Amazon also doesn't know, as this consumer continues to exist just as brightly in a constellation of shoppers as long as purchases are made. In Vuong's rendering, months without any purchases are still held open with blank space, marking time and the significant life we can choose to assume is lived between purchases. Are these gaps sorrowful or joyful? We can't be so sure they're only indicative of suffering, only that they represent a body meeting its needs in alternative ways. They may by months, unbeknownst or unimaginable to us, filled with ability, not despair, traces left elsewhere.

As a documentary work, Vuong's poem doesn't involve research per se but sources its language from a purportedly neutral source to perform this moving act of emotional journalism and accounting. In this way the poem revels in how close it *doesn't* get to life, or anything near the totality of a life, preserving mystery and privacy in this presentation, the suggestion of a closed world between mother and son into which we are not invited. We may infer the *what* of this poem, the who and how, but the particulate emotional muck remains opaque. Love can also be privacy, even in the telling of that love. Considering writers of color are constantly over-read for the "what happened" of their poems and subsequently under-read for their workmanship and formal innovation, it's also possible to experience Vuong's poem as a rejection of this phenomenon by declining emotional exposition, choosing instead to compose itself entirely of detritus, residual data. *I won't exactly tell you about it*, Vuong's poem seems to say, *but I'll show you the marks and stains left behind.*

Maybe: This documentary work instructively challenges that other phenomenon found in much of celebrity culture, from which literary culture is not totally separate, of para-social identification as the primary door into the work. It's ultimately an act of entitlement, masquerading (even to the reader themselves) as admiration, which elides much of the craft of the poem itself. In a social moment where everybody is capable of becoming their own brand, building out our tiny empires, the marketplace continues to reward a digestible and streamlined "relatable" narrative upon which the poem can float. Do readers want to imagine and stretch those imaginations, or do they want to "relate" in the sense of seeing themselves uncomplicatedly reflected in the work?

I'm using a distinction between these two modes of reading that borrows from Rebecca Mead's essay "The Scourge of Relatability," which takes as its catalyzing incident a viral tweet by the critic Ira Glass, in which he wrote, "Shakespeare sucks. Not relatable," a statement that he later retracted. Mead writes about the shifting definition of the word:

> Whence comes relatability? A hundred years ago, if someone said something was "relatable," she meant that it could be told—the Shakespearean sense of "relate"—or that it could be connected to some other thing. . . . The contemporary meaning of "relatable"—to describe a character or a situation in which an ordinary person might see himself reflected—first was popularized by the television industry.[8]

Vuong perhaps asks us to relate, or to watch the poem's attempt at relating, only in the Shakespearean sense, as in: Can this loss be *told*? Can it be connected to any other thing or experience that will clarify and calm it? Can it be compared, *said* via language at all? The poem's form seems to answer no, it can't, at least not with lyricism nor exposition, declining to try with either mode. This loss is thus not relatable, and the poem bold in its unrelatability. But what about in the newer sense of the word? Surely the poem imagines that readers have lost loved ones, have felt deep grief, battled cancer, or watched others lose that battle. For them, would the poem not offer any validating narrative or exposition, even a glimpse of redeeming beauty or epiphany? They who are so "ready" to "relate," to look into a mirror of their own grief? Vuong's poem seems to doubly reject this desire; after all, this grief should not *be*, is not wanted, and would not be wished upon any other. So why make it "relatable" at all?

Relatability is a poor metric for art in general, bordering on the absurd, as are claims to its close-behind friend, the metric of "universality." Mead, quoting David Masciotra writing on the literary website The Millions, gives us an example: "Karl Ove Knausgaard's account of his teen-age pursuits—drinking beer, kissing girls, playing electric guitar—in the 'My Struggle' novels is 'universally relatable.'"[9] *Sure it is*, Mead implies. Anecdotally, in my classrooms I often see the desire for easy relatability intensify para-social desire, escalated by an author's rising star. I read this as a natural (and troublesome) symptom of the Obama-era Representational Industrial Complex popular with middle-class liberalism—representation as liberation, and the attitudes that support that analysis. I'm thinking of the evergreen "Hire More Women Guards!" tweet[10] that so perfectly skewers the limited imagination and depravity of neoliberalism, as if the carceral state's cruelty can be fixed with more representation. Western militaries frequently tout their queer and female soldiers with the tone of a workplace recruitment pamphlet, signaling that the armed forces are a great and equitable place to work. We are seemingly supposed to agree: Isn't it better to be killed by a member of an oppressed class?

Vuong's poem seems to feel this representational anxiety and is animated by it, refusing narrative anchors and the naming of identity categories that may provide easy relatability by these hellish neoliberal metrics. Instead, we must enter the poem a different way, less assumptive or entitled, more experientially, through both sound and this realm of branded language and product. If there is any beauty to be found in the language it's accidental, the macabre lyric of capitalism that produces a neologism like Chemo-Glam. The poverty of needing representational (and identitarian) pleasure in order to move toward solidarity or imagination is brought into sharp and powerful relief.

The Amazon history-as-form is perhaps the most emblematic living archive[11] of our current moment, one created for us without consent or regard, for the purpose of profit growth and future attention capture. It is not *speech*, though it bears losses and scars. Amazon is a malevolent witness that witnesses nonetheless with its corrupt logic of capture and commerce. Repurposed as a poem, Vuong's vision is a subsequent witnessing, corrective though equally marred, movingly and painfully so.

Coda

Last night in front of a large group of graduate students, I asked what grief is, and is it a past-facing force? Or is it one of futurity? What does it look like on the page? Our conceptualizations and neater metaphors failed us right away. It's an absence surely, but then why is it heavy like a stone? It's a hole, but why do we feel *full* of it? If it gives us the power to time travel, in which direction should we *want* to go? It felt true to us that a ghost may be a balm until it hurts you, a nothingness that is everywhere. And what can language do for grief, we asked? Not much, it seemed. Language is neither a rescue mission nor a memorializing plaque; it heroically or stupidly attempts something doomed to fail. But we agreed, it seemed, that grief was "interesting." That we were in turn pleased to be *interested* in it as a *power*, as a generative force and had, in our own lived experiences, freely offered ourselves up to be stained by it. I thought later of Lyn Hejinian's claim that "form is not a fixture but an activity"[12] in describing the poem's rejection of closure and how that rejection is aided and abetted by such formal activity. Grief too is both act and activity. We wondered, not without anxiety, what traces of our own we wanted to leave intentionally, and if they would be as truthful as the story told by our accidental purchase histories and digital shards. Who would look for us if we didn't make it into the future intact?

Notes from the Writing of an Unwritten Novel

1. It's not a poem, it's a novel. That's the hard part. Don't forget.
2. You could introduce it: "Tank Man" is a novel about longing. It's named after the (unnamed) Beijing Tiananmen Square protestor of June 4, 1989, made iconic through a series of journalistic photos widely circulated in the aftermath of the massacre on the Square. In the decades since, the images are often used as a kind of visual shorthand (sometimes questionably or appropriatively) for collective struggle and resistance around the world. Tank Man's attempt to block the approach of a column of tanks sent to crush the student movement on Tiananmen Square resonates differently inside and outside of China, where the image has been systematically suppressed and censored,[1] such that many Chinese are unable to recognize an image of Tank Man or are unable to risk admitting that they do.[2]
3. "Tank Man" the novel-in-progress takes this very real historical event as well as its social, cultural, and political reverberations, and pulls from it a multi-POV fictionalized thread to explore a young woman's obsession with the past, and the particular immigrant fantasy of "return." The novel explores immigrant guilt, filial piety and obligation, and the fine lines between truth and belief, *both* of which work together to uphold the protagonist's precarious sense of identity forged in the United States in the aftermath of '89.
4. Yin is a Chinese American woman whose uncle was disappeared in the '89 massacre, a disappearance whose importance she has mythologized and elaborated in the decades since arriving in

America. Yin grows steadily unhappier with her life, her work, New York City, and begins to experience a series of terrifyingly cryptic dreams involving her uncle and grandfather. When a new trove of information about the events of '89 is suddenly released to the international public, and coveted by both the political and art worlds, Yin travels first to Shanghai and then to an unnamed village in the South of France to question everything she thought she knew about her life, her sanity, and the ideological role of the artist as a participant in history's highest-stake narratives.

5. The thing about Yin is she's been doing this all her life. Taken other people's stories, their memories, and lived them as if they were her own. It doesn't matter if this makes her more of a poet or a novelist, because Yin is not a writer.
6. Yin thinks Tank Man was her uncle; is it true? (you should probably decide). It's shaped Yin's life and her sense of "what she escaped." Is it true?
7. Immigrant stories are half-truths with a cauterizing effect. Maybe Yin's mom is a prolific liar like your own.
8. Immigration breaks bonds, stories, families.
9. A little ekphrasis then: He held two white shopping bags, one in each hand, as he moved his body to block the approach of the lead tank. His clothing was not that of a rich man, of that much everyone was sure. He transferred the bag from his right hand to his left hand as the lead tank continued its approach. He was young, and you didn't need to see his face to know it, where else would such impressive calm come from? Youth, stupidity, or idealism. He didn't move with an air of desperation or bravado—only a confounding steadiness, like a scene played one last time for the enraptured audience. An encore that the players rarely oblige. It seemed to all that he was already a ghost, brave as only the dead can be.
10. The thing about Elaine is, she's seen some shit. Immigration is the hinge in the dead center of her life, and when you've lived your own "before" you don't spend your "after" longing for it. She sees Tank Man as the highest-grade symbolism, pointless, mist.
11. The other thing about Yin is, the past is romantic.
12. You could tell people: Tank Man is informed greatly, though

certainly not exclusively, by my own immigration and the tight-knit community of Chinese American immigrants that raised me in the Midwestern United States. Our stories have been flattened and homogenized by both a news cycle uninterested in our particularities as well as a literary marketplace equally devoted to our tokenization. It's these intersecting processes that I work actively against, particularly in this novel project, which explores my long-standing literary fixations across genres of intergenerational inheritance, assimilation, immigrant female friendships, and "the past" as both a historical reality and a conceptually rich literary device. My project wants to reveal the invisible ways that immigration (which is itself not a homogeneous experience) plays out in the realm of the interpersonal, even mundane, between young Chinese American girls and the women they fight to become. Education and class stratification (on both sides of the ocean) further divide the experiences of these young female protagonists, and shape their relationship to an America which simultaneously beckons and rejects them.

13. The problem of research is the problem of documentation, when you say that the past exists and they say *where?* I'm sorry, this past is not a state-approved historical event. If the state has *feelings* about this non-event those can still be found, but must be inferred through what the state leaves out of the state's storytelling. The state will read you a bedtime story now!
14. Remember to look into the "little swallow song" that your mother sang to you, that plays in the background of all your early memories in this country. Where did it come from? Was it a real song that existed outside of your mother? Did it just come into being from her body? You remember that it was just one verse, and that you experienced deep identification with the "little swallow," and that "here" was clearly America, literally called "beautiful country" in Chinese:

    Little Swallow, wearing colorful feathers
    Returns here spring after spring
    I ask Little Swallow why they come
    Little Sparrow says because spring here is the most beautiful

Thus it seemed that your mother was reassuring you that you, too, would have beautiful recurring springs in America, and that to come here was reasonable, sane, and beautiful.

15. But "little swallow song" also has a disappeared past, an *unapproved* past voided by your mother. A second verse that she never sang, ghoulishly different:

    Little Swallow
    Let me tell you
    This year it will be even more beautiful here
    We have built big factories
    Installed new machines
    You are welcome
    To live here forever

    What to do with this ghost stanza from a revolutionary era propaganda children's song, meant as an explicit ode to industrialization? To realize your mother didn't write it for you, that it describes Chinese urbanization and the destruction of trees and land?
16. Did Tank Man ever hear this song? [serious question; unanswerable] That he too had a mother who might have sung to him about trees and land should not be described or manufactured; it's a poem unto itself.
17. Did Yin ever hear this song? [serious question; answerable]
18. "Little Swallow Song" was written by Wang Lu in 1956 for Children's Day; it was used in the 1957 Chinese mainland film *Diary of a Nurse*, and is sung by the main character to a sick child at bedtime.[3] It pacifies the child as it pacified you, a child that was often sick with misunderstanding and language-confusion in America.
19. Should you watch *Diary of a Nurse*? Do you want to watch it?
20. The fiction of "the good immigrant" or "the immigrant who fully overcomes trauma" is urgent and should be felt, as "Who is good?" is "Who is allowed to live?" in the world. Who is good in your world?
21. Is Yin good? [serious question; unanswerable]

Agoraphobe Logics

On Liu Xia, Agoraphobia, and Doubles

Seven Suppositions

1. As two figures of isolation, two types of pain, the agoraphobe and the house-arrested political prisoner. The agoraphobe luxuriates in barriers of a different kind, fences of the mind. In this way the agoraphobe is neuroses incarnate, a creature without rationality and on whom rationality (external rational acts) is lost.
2. The political prisoner is granted supreme rationality as a reward for her public suffering, her pain in exchange for our safety. Omelas, etc.[1] She radiates a pure, if cold, moral light. Does she love or resent us, her supporters? Would she embrace us or does she wish us to take her place?
3. Liu Xia, wife of the late poet and Nobel Peace laureate Liu Xiaobo, under house arrest for eight years, freed and now in exile in Berlin,[2] wrote often of dolls, birds, and cages. The house-arrested female poet suffers especially for being confined in the female space with which she is already familiar. She fears and longs for public space, the male space outside her home which is also surveilled space, as all public space is (surveilled; male). Thus to stay inside, the domestic female, the house-arrested female political prisoner, is further rational and worthy of our pity and love. It's all too clear what we want from the proud female prisoner, her inert tragic symbolism excites us. She litmus tests our empathy, that pointless feeling[3] that feels so good.
4. Does the agoraphobe have social, political, literary function? Does she *mean* at all beyond her irrationality and *dys*function?

Even her *dys*function may transform, in the event of the Covid-19 pandemic, into supreme rationality, and the agoraphobe may momentarily experience a position of the highest moral fortitude, a condition of loving others *this* much to be willing to shun the world, to stay inside. The political prisoner, it's possible, would gladly exchange our love for her freedom.

5. The agoraphobe uses carceral language to describe her condition, she is a prisoner, she is captive inside her body. She can't escape, she can't go outside, there is no condition of externality. It seems then that writing must become expulsion, escape. The urge to be expository, ejaculative, only when the other urges are muted, urges for poetry, for food, for rest, for sex, for figurative speech. She goes to Paris because she can, because her body goes with her and her *can't* is emotional not literal, and she medicates it into setting her free for an afternoon to sit by the water. The urge for poetry remains very faint, almost nonexistent, the writing is more diarrhetic and eliminatory.
6. Doll Logic: transforms you into a mother or a killer, your doll will never live and never die, she's inert or patient, she seethes with nightmarish potential or trad-fantasy. Her supreme innocence is off-putting, disgusting and endearing. Is she biding her stillness before enacting a horror? You've been given a doll because you're a woman, to learn to obey her monstrous needs. She's a preview or a replacement; replicant logic. She's your dead double or your perfect child.
7. Liu Xia's dolls, in her poetry and photography, scream and flail, hang precariously off surfaces, sit with their entire heads shrouded, are splayed on doors and rocks, stare out from beneath enormous Chinese characters, perform beneath hot stage lights, are attacked by leviathan hands. Their mouths open forever. Liu Xia is her husband's witness, inert and moral, dolls witness her captivity as she witnessed his. Witness Logic: don't flinch.

2020

Covid-19 didn't make me agoraphobic; it revealed my long-standing agoraphobe's logic to me. The disorder has been pathologized as everything from a product of Freudian sexual dysfunction to a symptom of the failures of modern city planning and architecture. Too many open spaces, too rapid urbanization, even a symptom of patriarchal forces in the lives of women and girls.[4] But agoraphobe logic as logic is entirely sound, and begins as a functional dislike of crowded, barren, or enclosed spaces, anywhere from which escape might be difficult or embarrassing, and the dignity of the agoraphobe might be compromised. It's nothing if not a dignity-loving logic. It's her belief in the probability of humiliation and its consequences that are outsized, even disastrous. She engineers her life and habits to attempt to cultivate the exact certainty that all human beings must learn to live without. Her rituals and possessions are safety checks to manifest the sensation of *guarantee*.

In 2020 those of us alive on earth encountered a fundamentally inverse agoraphobic dilemma, one in which a rational agent would engineer her life however possible to avoid an invisible threat, inherently a social threat because it is borne by other people and through contact. Her belief in the consequences of acting against an agoraphobic logic is not outsized, is the material loss of life. While rereading Liu Xia's *Empty Chairs*[5] during the pandemic, I found myself unintentionally thinking of the house-arrested political prisoner as also having an agoraphobic experience engineered by state repression. Cruelly, the prisoner is made to assist the state apparatus by jailing herself due to threat, both psychic and physical, in a domestic world engineered to be as small as possible. It is rational and in the interest of self-preservation, of a kind, to stay inside. A complex tangle of nationalistic authorizations and capitalist patent laws amounting to vaccine apartheid guaranteed that in 2021, while nations in the Global North began to take the first Covid-19 vaccines, much of the rest of the world remained vulnerable, shunted into an endless 2020 with its prevailing agoraphobic rules.

"Your Mediocre Wife"

The agoraphobe experiences that each person going about their business in the world is her happier double, a classic doppelgänger story of one blessed twin and the dark Other, locked in the proverbial basement while the happier double inhabits the social and thus male world. He moves freely in both physical and political space, while the agoraphobe is affectively female, mute. Liu Xia's poem "Scheme" (1988) describes the dissatisfaction of writing and being known in writing, seeing it not as a form of physical or emotional agency, but rather a dissociative state leading to "despair, even madness." Liu Xia casts writing as ultimately a visitation or possession, a lonely male force which moves according to its own whims in her name:

> Poems with my name
> on them pile up,
> but you don't know it's a scam.
> A lonely soul, a guest,
> comes now and then and moves my pen.
> He likes my writing
> and the way I smoke.[6]

Liu Xia's vision of authorship is either bleak or lucid, suggesting that even a prolific output of poetic speech is just a scam, a ventriloquism for her more talented double. "When I'm alone with him, / my words are tidy and beautiful." With inspiration comes expectation, and Liu Xia dreams of shirking off her visitor who makes her accumulate attention as an author:

> I want to give up my name as a poet.
> It makes others expect things from me
> and makes me face the blank page
> with despair, and even madness.[7]

Throughout, the poet resists and outright resents a romanticization of her poetry writing as having political power, even as her husband Xiaobo's persecution (and thus hers by proxy) by the Chinese state was largely due to his writing, and his poetry in particular. Jailed for eleven years due to a long history of pro-democracy activism and criticism of the Chinese state, including signing the Chinese dissident manifesto "Charter 8" in 2008, Liu Xiaobo looms large as both political intellectual and agitator. For Liu Xia, he looms large first as husband, later as absence. It would be reductive to read the poem's ambiguous "he" as *only* Liu Xiaobo, but nonetheless it includes him, and Liu Xia casts herself as the ineffectual half of their twinned relationship. "I can only live in this room," she writes, shifting to direct address, "be your mediocre wife, / shop, cook, and do laundry, / or light a cigarette / and stare out the window for a long time." Xiaobo and the specter of poetry are themselves inextricably twinned as visiting angels from the social masculine world out of doors:

> His world is too far—
> Farther than I can reach
> in this life.[8]

A poem written ten years after "Scheme," "Misplaced" contains yet more overt imagery of seeing oneself as a double, closer to astral projection (projected consciousness) than dissociation:

> Fragile and unprepared, I've been tossed
> into a play with no dress rehearsal.
>
> Betrayed by the shimmering lights,
> I see myself standing on the stage
> in an absurd posture; I see
> the fool's sharp teeth gleaming.
>
> The character, assumed
> sad and weak,
> loses control: her hungry veins
> burst into surging waves.
> So I become a red-eyed evil witch,
> and, under watchful eyes,
> brew wine inside skulls[9]

Here Liu Xia plays with valences of performativity and thus falsehood and artifice using a stage metaphor, where the doppelgänger Other is simply "the character" before repossessing the "I" through a transformative hunger. Fragility alchemizes into a cautious power ("under watchful eyes") through hunger, necessity, and duress. "No costumes or makeup / can disguise me," she writes,

When the show is over,
I stay on stage with myself:
one of me is tearful
the other laughing loudly.[10]

A mitosis is complete, and the doubles consider each other in a clever reference to the dialectical masks of Tragedy and Comedy. "Misplaced" is a poem general (and generous) enough in language and metaphor to speak to common experiences of being misunderstood or forced to perform a role, but the context of the house-arrested political prisoner adds a dimension of necessity to generalized (read: coded, plausibly deniable) language. You might call this an agoraphobe's logic as well, an engineering of the environment (in this case the poem) to manifest safety where none exists. An extreme fixation on achieving it. If the agoraphobe is paranoid it is the same paranoia as the surveilled political prisoner but without "reason," though the agoraphobe would disagree. The efficacy of surveillance as an element of statecraft hinges on this exact paranoia in order for surveilled subjects to police themselves, having no way to rationally determine what punishments might be visited upon them for what actions. By design, the only guarantee of safety is to behave as the agoraphobe would.

Code or Confession

"I live in the bodies of the dolls / who kill themselves over and over in dreams"[11] begins the poem "It's Only Waking Up," from 1999. A short three-stanza poem about the tedious cycle of living ("When I wake up / I find myself not reborn / but only waking up"), Liu Xia's poem employs dolls again as doubles, suggesting darkly that it is only because the doubles can kill themselves repeatedly in dreams, promising even a possibility of a profound rebirth, that the speaker is able to keep on living herself. The dolls are both sacrificed children and a never-ending suicide for a speaker who sits "alone with a single light at night / feeling guilty / and grateful / at the same time," evoking either an interrogation room or a single nightlight of comfort. This pointed ambiguity leads to the poem's final haunting image of threat, paranoia, and desire:

Wind has been blowing the curtains,
but who can prove
it's just the wind?[12]

Liu Xia's poems are often looking over their shoulder, for obvious reasons, and her encapsulation of the paranoia of life under surveillance is never more distilled and vivid than in this final stanza. This image's double is, of course, a bittersweet fantasy (cruel optimism) of wishing for a loved one to return home, for if the rustle at the curtain isn't them, at least a sign of life borne on the wind. Because it's *both*, not neither, the poem contains its own alibi against accusations of dissent or worse, the smuggling into public of news of the house-arrested political prisoner's lived conditions. Doubling and ambiguity, then, become a form of safety here, and allow the poem's confession of suffering.

*Un*doubled and *un*coded speech is both Liu Xiaobo's privilege and sin, for which he was sentenced to eleven years in Chinese state prison before passing away in state custody. In 2009, Liu Xia wrote in an untitled poem dedicated to her husband,

You speak and speak and speak the truth.
You speak day and night, as long as you're awake
you speak and speak.
Your voice breaks free from the sealed room and disperses.
. . . .
You love your wife and are proud she stays with you
through the darkness; you let her do what she wants, write for you
even after death, but in her verses there are no sounds. None.[13]

The image of Liu Xia as the soundless and ineffectual double returns in this poem, written both in praise and subtle condemnation of her husband's irrepressible speech, always clear and plausibly *un*deniable, in defiance of the Chinese government. The poem repeats "You speak" eighteen times in total, a litany of accusation. In 2020, I felt even more certain that a poem was a way to go outward, not further into myself to mine for highlights of self. Together with students, I found that our poems longed for certainty and reassurance while taking careful inventory of the staggering external unknowns we were living. It's not that the mysteries of ourselves dimmed, but the mysteries of our fragile bond with others glowed brighter. We repeated our assertions of *you* exist, and this knowledge must mean that I exist too. Some days we felt we were the "fragile and unprepared" twin, "tossed / into a play with no dress rehearsal."[14] And yet we spoke and spoke and spoke, we hope, the truth.

Monologue on Intention

2014–2017

I apologized to the composer by saying that I did not intend to be such a literalist, and perhaps I had misunderstood the invitation to collaborate. I didn't wake up wanting to misunderstand. I didn't come here to get it wrong. I couldn't see past the objects of my own misinterpretation.

The genre that I intended to critique was my own. I was unsatisfied with its parameters and set about remaking them to suit my needs. I don't think I lied to anyone, though it's possible that I did. Genres are like gods, I don't believe in them, but they hang over me anyway. Unmoved by my disbelief.

When I called you, you said you intend to edit me, but you didn't specify further. Into what?

When the good Iowa farm boy, the boy who sat next to me in class leaned over and called me a chink, I might have said back, "Please let me know the intention here." What is my role here, my next move as scripted by you? Where do I enter this knowledge of myself? And where does pain enter me? When the good boy stood up I let him know that his message had been received. I let him know that he need not answer.

The ambiguity may not have been what you intend, but it moves like a vapor or a cloud around us. Your intention races your desire, and both come out on top. You might have even written it down somewhere. When I was twelve I went with my mother to the supermarket, and we were heckled by another child somewhere in the produce aisle. He couldn't believe us and would not try. We were choosing vegetables for dinner beneath the ASIAN FLAVORS sign. I had snuck a copy of *Mad* magazine into our shopping cart, hoping that my mother wouldn't notice. She kept saying that we were not the ones being heckled, it was not for us and shuffled me quickly toward the checkout line.

I sure hope it seems as simple to you as I intend for it to. I've tried to diagnose your questions and address them in real time. I've worked to avoid your inability to relate.

How do you intend for this to work?

That's a good question. I can't remember what I intend for my poetry to do these days. Of course, I guess it's not really my problem. It will do what it wants to do. What will I be doing?

I do not intend my demands, but I've made them anyway. They're flaccid in that way, and you can pick one up and hold it or you can kick it into the gutter. When I asked to be paid, something weird and cold moved through the body of my loved one. It was illegible to me but I gave it space. When they asked my father to recite the Pledge of Allegiance, he may or may not have mumbled the parts he couldn't remember. Nobody got hurt. Nobody even knew.

The application form asked me to write that I intend to be the kind of teacher who intends to be in the classroom. One of the problems in my life is that being in the classroom leaves my body vulnerable. I once asked a male colleague if he ever felt self-conscious about his body while writing on the blackboard. I said, "Do you feel safe with eyes on your body?" to which he responded that yes he did, and that in fact one of his refrains in the classroom was "All eyes on me!" to which I laughed, and I don't think he knew why.

I intend to do, I intend to be, keep being, and at the end of the day I'm exhausted by the distance between the train station and my apartment because I'm full of sadness and occasionally the feeling of unfulfilled potential.

My mother is certain that they don't intend anyone to know that we live here, we're such a blemish at the PTA meetings and we declare ourselves too much, we're so aggressively odd and the stink of us hangs long after the barbecue is over. I go to babysit three angelic boys down the street, the parents are kind and their regular babysitter is busy, they are desperate to have a night out, I'm fifteen and I get a nosebleed right after dinner all over their lily-white couch, they have to come home from the movie and they pay me anyway. The children help me clean up the stain with toilet paper and vinegar.

Sometimes I tell people that I haven't read that but I intend to, and if they're listening, really listening, they might hear that beneath it I am saying I will never read it, though I don't know that this is what I'm saying, and they'll forgive me for it anyway. To unwillingly read undermines the intentions of the poem, the poet's intention to be read with love.

They will like to hear that you intend to bring some of that creative energy to the position.

I tell the clerk that he should not speak to my mother like that, fluster her with his English in front of all these people, I'm twelve and I don't like to be embarrassed by my mother's embarrassment, and I can't see beyond the smallness of my desire. I'm afraid of the completion of the circle of your intent. I have only the best and they arrange themselves across my vision as to form a complete partition. Some days I can't touch my family.

Reading that over now it sounds like I was trying to talk down to you, which was not my intention.[1]

Disappear Yourself

Unsayability in Henri Michaux and Chase Berggrun

I used to believe that more of the world, including much of my own experience in it, was *sayable*, able to be depicted. My own immigration, a subject I often wrote about, must be wholly articulable, via great effort and above all precision on my part. That it was, as we sometimes say, a "craft" issue, and a craft challenge. Though I must have said and depicted much in the last ten years, most of it with seriousness and care, I'm less sure than ever about what is utterable.

Of course we have the idiom of something rendering one "speechless," which is sometimes literal but more often shorthand for being so surprised or shocked that one can't find the *right* speech, the correct combo to get at describing *it*, or the state that learning *it* has brought one to. I'm rarely speechless myself because I dislike processing my experiences silently in my head; I often get speech*ful* when surprised, or confused, or devastated. Experiences of tragedy have more than once resulted in an immediate abundance of speech.

It's been generative for me to decide to go to the page more often in response to language-resistant experiences. Can I go *there*, to the friction between my wanting to say and my limited tools for saying? Sometimes what finds me, compellingly, and easily, is language for my frustration with this friction, so that I must narrate my own struggle to overcome this essential lack. Sometimes all this saying and trying to say makes me feel disappeared, submerged beneath a surface of language, like ice on a frozen lake. Looking for a little hole through which to surface. The struggle of depiction leaves me cold like this, frustrated, where in the past it would have made my memories feel more alive. I'm not entirely sure what explains this change. But so much *saying* makes the past feel deadened somehow, or is it overly polished, so that all its interesting unsayable roughnesses must be ground down?

My life was halved in 1989, when my family came in America. I live thus in the post-, and can never return to the pre-. I feel it as a cut, a death, and a birth, the most dialectical experience that I live out daily. In all these years of trying to articulate my halves poetically and artistically, I've found myself behaving and evaluating scientifically, searching for the empirical evidence that I exist, that my life can be tested and found true through the depiction and proofing of details in language. I feel as if my poems are conditioned to test themselves for accuracy under constant threat of being subjected to worse tests. The more freely I've tried to depict, the less free I feel to speak, when the stakes are my life.

I'm reluctant to wonder aloud if the world, and the things we do in it, are becoming more "unsayable," because I'm not interested in comparing the atrocities and beauties of one age with another. Surely we have always suffered, killed, loved, been awed. Sought and found sublime and speechless experiences across all of time. But much *is* unsayable in our time, more so *denied* saying by the institutions and loci of power that produce Official Speech. Speech or it didn't happen, etc. And this withheld speech, a form of which is passive speech, denies entire realities, cultural histories, genocides, violent ideologies. The passive voice *kills*, literally, or at least it would admit that it kills were it not busy saying that the other party *was killed*. The depravity of the *New York Times*' coverage of the bombardment of Gaza starting in October 2023 is a masterclass in such cruel decoupling of speech and reality, perpetuated by the passive voice. Active verbs carry their ideologies on their sleeve, as only Palestinians "slaughter," or "massacre," while the "war" in Gaza passively "turns Gaza into a Graveyard for Children."[1] Even in this seemingly sympathetic headline, the characterization of "graveyard" is borrowed from the United Nations. Hundreds more of these examples abound, published anew every day. To be "speechless" is increasingly less a condition of finding oneself in the grip of awe, but a political category of erasure engineered by violent passivity. The nation-state, it seems, is never speechless—it is always engaged with creating ideal conditions for its own speech to flourish.

Thus it seems urgent to try to speak against speechlessness and the supposedly unsayable, doomed as the effort might be. To practice that speaking daily, and to make a habit of attempting when the opportunity presents itself. When I consider the formalization of an effort like this, I think of Henri Michaux's famous mescaline experiments and the writing and drawings it produced, collected neatly for English-language readers in *Miserable Miracle*.[2] Michaux's interest in altered states and consciousnesses is well documented, in this case by the author himself, as was the general interest among his mid-century symbolist and surrealist peers. The project is charmingly earnest bordering on comedic, to approach mescaline and its effects with the controlling hand of a scientist, aiming to quantify and record with empirical precision what mescaline produces in the mind. Notably, Michaux's project has been praised for being "devoid of either superficial moralizing or unfounded hyperbole,"[3] unique in this regard among his peers, filled instead with ecstatic and sometimes laboriously careful efforts to correctly and fully capture each wave of powerful mescaline hallucinations. That it does not necessarily transport a reader, sound of mind and herself not under the influence of mescaline, to an altered reality, is not the fault of Michaux or his sentences. But the project's irrational (perfectly so) optimism about the possibility of really *saying* mescaline in such a way that would transcend the sobriety of the page is, for me, its utopian heart.

The most evocative of Michaux's mescaline *drawings* contain wonderful visual contradiction, appearing to be both microscopic and cosmic at once, like a flake of human skin beneath a microscope that is also an eagle's eye view of an alien landscape. Many are viscerally bisected by a jagged split, like watching a scab open up into a canyon; when I peer in, I feel sudden permission to leave all my sorrows down there in the pit. Is it me or Michaux that's feeling existential here? I can read, in his drawings, the pressure applied to the pen, focused from forearm to wrist and down through two flexed fingers, the pen tip responding to each renewed push, the paper bearing puncture in a particularly spirited moment, the insistence of the dark running back over itself until saturation. Some drawings in particular speak pain, suffering, ecstasy. Desire for pain to leave the body and flow out through the ink, repetition when pain doesn't abide. Where I lose this ability to "read" Michaux is the moment I perceive a drawing to look *like* a known thing—when simile finds me the image calcifies on the page. It is now an almost-rock, an almost-pine tree, and *reading* as an active process is closed to me. Emotion seems to drain from the image itself.

The language of *Miserable Miracle* relies heavily on exclamation, declaration of sensation and named emotion, fragments of sensory description, and the optimism of a well-selected adjective. Sentences cascade and revise themselves as they muck their way through the shifting hallucination, struggling to keep up. In one passage of enormous sensation and emotion, lost in the color pink, Michaux's efforts are earnest, insufficient, comical, even noble in their belief in the ability to put speech to pink's qualities. Michaux writes,

> Pink then not pink, then pink, then not pink, or barely pink, then very pink. Pink spreads. Innumerable pink bulbs appear. Pink spreads more and more. I generate it, I sparkle with it. I am sprouting pink. I suffocate with pinkness, with pinkening. The pecking of this pink disturbs me, is odious.
>
> Cessation.
>
> Thank heaven!

And in a marginal annotation for this passage, Michaux embraces the solution of more succinct poeticism: "In the pink sewer."[4] More distilled and assured compared to the tortured description of pink's ephemeral pinkness, it will have to do. What kind of pink? Ultimately, a sewer full. Description necessitates comparison, simile, chains of likes that Michaux is only able to avoid when he turns away from language completely and begins to draw. The drawing *is* the impression of the unsayable *it*, its truer mark, and asserts its relation directly.

I love a particular series of Michaux's drawings the best, which I'll called the grapho-lingual series where lines of aspirational text, sensual yet chaotic, slowly dissolve and dis-cohere into illegible strands and approximations of movement that drip down the page.[5] Though as soon as I assert this order of things, I wonder: Is language dissolving into nonsense, or are sentient lines struggling against their own illegible nature to cohere into language? Which way are things moving? Did someone fall asleep, while writing, with pen in hand? Or did a sleeper awake, with pen in hand, possessed with sudden urgency to record a frenetic dream? These drawings have a whiff of language, both playful and frustrating for it, but a reluctance to ultimately cohere into "sense." Barthes, writing on relatedly "illegible" paintings by André Masson, helpfully suggests that it is exactly the illegibility of illegible texts that makes them "true," and not just functional or instrumental.[6] Their earnestness is perhaps due to their effortfulness, the unabashed urge to overcome the unutterable that feels so human. Are we seeing a mutation photographed mid-change? And in this metaphor, what is the *natural* state? One of languaged existence, or wild illegibility? To call Michaux's grapho-lingual drawings *calligrams* seems somewhat suitable but undercutting of their powerful reluctance to deliver a stable image.

Michaux was deeply inspired by Chinese calligraphy from his earliest works of art, famously in *Alphabet* (1925), a project of "asemic" writing that appropriates the visual conventions of ideograms to produce impossible letters, impossible both to read and to replicate, while also moving in a "Western" method across the page, lines running left to right and down the page.[7] Logographic pleasures abound, rich and visceral. *Alphabet* is both opaque and engaging, soliciting our projection and participation as easily as it mocks our desire to decipher and truly *read* this imaginary text. Between language and image is something wilder, the dream of a third form transcending sayable experience.

Do ecstasy and despair disturb language the same? Surely pleasure sends out different ripples across language than fear, patterning the surface of speech anew. If fear sets itself *against* speech, against even the possibility of disclosure, what then? The *un*utterable in *R E D* by Chase Berggrun,[8] a book-length erasure project of Bram Stoker's *Dracula*, is both the isolating experience of sexual violence *and* the ecstatic momentum of gender transition and reclamation of bodily agency. Remade out of the misogynistic graveyard of Stoker's Victorian novel, *R E D*'s irrepressible "I" becomes "unsayable" in overlapping ways, first as a captive, assaulted and *said* (spoken) *for*, repeatedly visited by male violence. As she becomes, of all things, a writer out of necessity ("As I go mad / I write down / the little things"),[9] her unsayability becomes a problem of depiction, how to put down the reality of her world? Is there language *enough* for such suffering? And in the book's final act, truly an *act* of *unspeakable* power and agency takes place, a woman becoming such a menace to her captor that she cannot be named, described, or understood. She cannot be *said* any longer.

Many of erasure poetry's most insightful critics are also its practitioners, such as Solmaz Sharif, Robin Coste Lewis, and Berggrun herself, who has spoken in public about erasure's limits and risks,[10] and who also regularly teaches erasure poetry's long history. To try one's hand at "erasing" an existing text is to participate in violence of varying intensities. Methodology may differ and imply rescue or burial, the airlifting out of a word with surgical precision, or the brutality of redaction that forever entombs the censored text beneath black bars. Both produce an erasure text, and both require variations on verbs like cut, lift, remove, bury, snip, erase. This is physical work, visceral work, and it gives life in the same way a necromancer does—or if you prefer, the way God himself did by breaking off and enchanting Adam's rib. Perhaps Stoker's rib is similarly appropriated here, transformed into a queer and ravenous Eve, or is it Stoker's reanimated corpse that we're faced with?

Of course, Stoker's novel is the material reason *R E D* as a book is utterable at all, the textual body sacrificed so *R E D* can speak. Though Berggrun's interests are not in admiring, rehabilitating, or even litigating *Dracula*'s Victorian politics, *R E D* so coolly antagonizes its source text with an agile diction that hardly feels constrained, a transformation that might suggest a "I don't even think of you at all" attitude. Playful and cutting, there seems something inherently *femme* about this manner of relation to its monstrous male parent. To fashion oneself as best as allowed under constraint, to "work with what you've got" (as they say) literally, to make one's way with a new unapproved language in a man's world, all are *affectively* female conditions in a society deeply stratified by gender. This language's irrepressibility under duress further marks it *femme*, the revolt of an underclass speech.

The cruelty of *R E D*'s looming He is both sayable and not, drawing forth much writing from the speaker but seemingly unable to be narrated with anything but *figurative* language, suggesting that the full intensity of naming these violences is unbearable. Instead he "mutilate[s] [her] tenderness / He had stolen so much," the speaker writes, and of his body and bearing she offers that "[t]here was a mortuary air about him."[11] She asks plainly, "Is there something in woman that makes a man feel free to break her."[12] As this speaker takes unto herself more and more rage, experiencing repeated cruelties, "[Her] sweetness turned / to adamantine cruelty / purity to wantonness / obedient to nothing / an angry snarl / the remnant of [her] love / passed into savage delight" when she decides, with finality, to "strike the blow that sets me free."[13] Violence begets violence, a truth as old as our oldest stories. But on this speaker's way to becoming a force unrecognizable to her sadistic husband, she must (ironically or fittingly) pass through states of extreme speech, of prodigious self-declaration. She must, in fact, become the writer that she is. A wretched or blessed identity, but in *R E D*'s world a state of agency and power. Writing too can beget violence, and *R E D*'s speaker quickly turns to plotting:

> I threw grief-written lines all over my papers
> I studied the necessity of no remorse
> Survived long centuries as an inmate
> Alone and hidden in the ground
> I hastened towards the moment
> I care for nothing now except brute action
> It will take thousands of men to hold me back
> I had been accustomed to obey
> Now the old habit was just a nightmare.[14]

Writing, as a state of feverish imagination and optimism, is at odds with remorse, inaction, and morality, and notably depicted as inciting an explicitly female act, one equal to "thousands of men." "Why are men so little worthy of a girl,"[15] our speaker asks elsewhere. Why indeed.

The most writerly characteristic of *R E D*'s heroine is also her most femme: her relentless "I" in all states, meek or rageful, her refrain of self-knowledge situating her in the world and in sanity. Berggrun builds her heroine "I" by "I," stacking these pronouns potently even as they are characterized by their constrictive circumstances. In a single passage, such declaration: "I tidied myself . . . I was trying . . . I gave myself away . . . I have tried . . . I have copied out the words."[16] Against disappearance, and toward the goal of ridding herself of her husband, this heroine must declare and *say* herself as many times as possible. Without a name, she only exists as often as she can appropriate another first person from Stoker's text. A reader is often left with the sensation that much urgency lies in not knowing how many more opportunities Stoker's text will allow. And indeed, as Berggrun reminds us both inside and outside of a Victorian novel, when a woman dares utter herself too often, she bears incalculable risk, and wields incalculable power.

Part Two

Things to Do with Form

Wanted and Unwanted Forms

Think about your life. What shapes, forms, patterns, conventions, routines, power dynamics, and relationships inform it? These can be literal (e.g., an application form you fill out for a job) or more abstract (e.g., the awkward conversational pattern you've fallen into with a coworker). Make a two-column list, title one column "Wanted Forms" and the other "Unwanted Forms." Fill the list out as plentifully as you can. Include all sorts of things that come to mind. For example, the shape of the route you walk to school every day. Wanted? Unwanted? The form of the invasive interview for an immigration application. Wanted? Unwanted? The delicate and intricate politesse of small talk when you meet someone for the first time. Some may fall into both columns. Forms of writing that you like. Societal conventions you hate. Expectations, social roles, burdens and pleasures of custom. All forms.

Play around with your list of "Wanted" and "Unwanted" forms from your life that you've been compiling, and choose the most interesting one from each column that you want to transform into a brand-new *poem* form, complete with rules, parameters, and its own logics. Any poem can take any form, but why should it? How will it emote? Surely nobody will stop you from writing "a poem in the form of an email" or "a poem in the form of a conversation between a parent and child" but why? Know this for yourself, and for the poem. Know inside your heart. Will you find or source the language, or will it be original? Will it be drawn just from your own head? Why? How will it be restricted, and how will it be free? More importantly, can you love a form you didn't want? If once it hurt, can you make it heal? If once it surveilled, repressed, restricted, marginalized, can you (and do you want to?) renew it?

Read Bhanu Kapil's *How to Wash a Heart.*[1] Read Ocean Vuong's poem "Amazon History of a Former Nail Salon Worker."[2] Read Sarah Jean Alexander's poem "Please Eat."[3] Read Amber Atiya's Poem "New York State Office of Temporary and Disability Assistance SSI/Food Stamp Benefits Application."[4]

Banish Language

Banish language for the next thirty minutes. Draw a poem. If it helps you to imagine that you inhabit a postapocalyptic world, one where language has "failed" or become insufficient, do that. This might remind you a lot of the world you live in now, where daily language is used to obfuscate, harm, and justify. Look at some paintings, drawings, or photographs that you like. Remind yourself there are languages without words. Start with simple shapes that mean something to you, that please you emotionally or aesthetically. Collage or add existing images if you want, photography or clip-art or magazine clippings, any visual artifacts that belong.

Narratives in Time

Visit a museum in person, if you can. Any kind, it doesn't need to be an art museum. As you wander around, consider the *act* of curation, the human hands and minds that created this categorical language, these groupings, labels, associations, logics, and narratives. Read Robin Coste Lewis's introduction to her long poem "Voyage of the Sable Venus," and then read "Voyage of the Sable Venus," composed entirely of the titles and descriptions of artworks depicting a Black female figure throughout history.[5] Consider the anthropological gaze of the "Hall of Asian Peoples" and the "Hall of African Peoples" at the Museum of Natural History in NYC. Consider the mannequins depicting Asian and African peoples frozen in time in those halls.

Try for yourself, in a small but illuminating way, to see through some of the stories you're being fed. Choose a thing, place, or person that you are interested in that has been depicted in art. This could be simply "cats," or "airplanes," or "grandmothers" or "Beijing," anything that you think has likely been depicted in art across a long period of time. Then visit the websites of a few museums, three or four is good, and search up depictions of what you've chosen, noticing language, labels, groupings, subtexts.

Any patterns? Any recurrences? What are the stakes of the presentation? Any subtexts or distortions or gaps? What cultural fears or anxieties are being stoked across a long narrative, crossing centuries? Perhaps what you're seeing is unserious, but the methodology here must be taken very seriously. Humor is OK. Humor will not obscure the stakes of what you're trying to see.

Perhaps cats are overwhelmingly depicted as vicious, or the city of Beijing is always presented as smoggy. Surely they are sometimes this way. Who cahoots with whom in these presentations? Write your own curatorial statement. Make it as true as you can.

Poem with a Hole in It

Write a poem with a hole in it, literally. How else you define that is up to you, such as what shape the hole might be (round, large, small, sharp, menacing, blurred, layered), and what metaphorical "hole/loss" you want to manifest. Holes are also cuts, wounds, ghosts, portals back in time, portals forward in time, fault lines, weapons, openings, and possibilities. Explore the kind of hole you're interested in right now.

Two Environmental Poems

Consider some poems that feel and/or look like physical environments to you. Start with whatever is on your own bookshelf. Some other recommendations are M. NourbeSe Philip's *Zong!*,[6] Henri Michaux's mescaline drawings from *Miserable Miracle*,[7] Philip Metres's *Sand Opera*,[8] Sean Bonney's *Baudelaire in English*,[9] Stéphane Mallarmé's *The Book*,[10] Diana Khoi Nguyen's *Ghost Of*,[11] giovanni singleton's *American Letters: Works on Paper*,[12] Nicole Sealey's *The Ferguson Report: An Erasure*,[13] Layli Long Soldier's "Resolution" poems from *Whereas*,[14] and Mai Der Vang's *Yellow Rain*.[15] Now draw two boxes, to be filled with two new poems that feel "environmental" to you. Both poems will be contained within their environments (the boxes) . . . though of course they might escape . . . or strain their boundaries . . . or play with transgression as a form of energy . . .

You may write, draw, paste, cut, type, collage, color, stain, wrinkle, embroider, redact, set on fire, spill, whatever you want, but the resulting pieces must still primarily "exist" within the two environments. These two environmental poems also must be oppositional, such as Chaos/

Order, or Hot/Cold, etc., and they will be named as such. Will they be harmoniously opposite, like yin and yang, or will they defy each other? How does a poem aware of its environmentally bounded nature behave? How should it?

Who Knows?

Find an old poem you wrote and reread it, re-remembering the sensory experience of writing that poem if you can. Choose three of the most emotionally charged moments to change from a statement to a question. Simply add the question mark (?) to create this new moment. It doesn't need to be at the end of a line or phrase or sentence, it can be something like:

> And then you took my hand > And then you? took my hand

Then, reread your poem again, and picture the person you were when you wrote it. Add in three unanswerable questions that you want to ask to the person you were when you wrote it. This can be something like:

> Where did that green kite really disappear to?

Add the questions in, knowing that the poem can't answer, but you can. How does it feel to let these bursts of "unknowing" into the poem, to let it both rupture and revise the past like this? If you feel some sorrow for your poem as it was, that's OK. Feel that most of all.

Friends and Enemies

Grab a friend, this one requires two minds. Write two postcards (each of you), one to an enemy and one to a loved one. Write as truthfully, painfully, spitefully, tenderly, as you want. Name or don't name their recipients, it's not important. Exchange postcards. Give each other permission (this part *is* important) to chop up and erase the other's postcards.

Using your friend's postcard to an enemy, erase and rearrange and cut-up words until it sounds loving, tender even. Using your friend's postcard to a loved one, erase and rearrange and cut-up words until it sounds venomous and upset. Read your two new resulting poems to each other, and find time to laugh and marvel at the uncanny transformations. Talk about how you feel, especially if discomfort creeps into your experience of cutting up your friend's words.

What Will Happen Tomorrow?

Write a new poem that tries to answer the question "What will happen tomorrow?" with a list of wrong answers, made-up possibilities, longed-for outcomes, and impossible images. Devise a new form for your poem that feels "precognitive" to you. What is a knowing form?

Absence Speaks

Does absence speak louder than words? Try to make it. Write a brand-new poem in any form where the absence on the page speaks louder than the words on it. Your poem must use both (absence and words), but how you define these is up to you. Your absence could be subject, for example, but not evident in the technique. Maybe a person or feeling or memory is gone . . . and their absence is much more felt than the words themselves would even like to believe. Or, your poem might be visually riddled with literal holes, gaps, or what the translator of Sappho's fragments Anne Carson calls "lacks," and these gone-nesses might seem to be shouting over the actual words on the page. You might end up with a monologue, a transcript, a script, a prose paragraph, some stanzas, a fragment, a collage, an essay, a fiction, a character sketch, an ekphrasis, a response to a memory, a set of lyrics, or something else entirely.

Poem by Heart

Start to freewrite and describe a memory that you "know by heart," as they say, although surely there are other ways to know. But for now, something you've told backward and forward, meaningful and enduringly resonant in some way, don't overthink what "way" that is exactly, and add all of the details and colors and sensations you can think of.

Now start to write describing yourself in medias res sitting in your real environment, describing and remembering the memory as you are.

Think of this as adding, suddenly and willfully, your extreme presence, your body, your self from which all memory is drawn, creating a memory itself as it writes.

Next describe a hole or absence or detail from the memory that you don't actually remember, letting the hole reveal itself, how long it's been there, give it significance by describing it, drawing it forward, acknowledging that you don't know what you don't know, but you do know that you don't know, and that's something . . . it has edges and you can trace them.

Finally, write in first person *as* the absence or missing detail speaking from somewhere else, from where it has gone—where has it gone? How long has it been gone? What is it like *there* in the place that it has made for itself? What does it want, what does it want to tell you? What does it think of this story you've just finished telling without it?

Five Questions, Five Statements

Think of a real place from your past or present that has the aura of a question mark to you. You don't have to explain *why* to anybody, but maybe this is a place that feels unfinished, unknown, confusingly resonant, attractive, or mysterious. Write five questions addressed to that place, whatever feels right to ask. Now think of a place that feels like a period, demarcated, ended, heavy with closure. Write five statements addressed to this place. Weave these lines together and let them converse, challenge, or compliment each other.

Three Fragments

Let us not fetishize wholeness, cohesion, which is related to palatability, neatness, linearity, legibility. Let us also not readily believe that fragmentation and fracture are neutral and naturally occurring processes. Sometimes what breaks off inside of or from us is sharp, shard-ed, and it doesn't cease to exist, it becomes sentient and outlives us. Read Kazim Ali's "The 'Tradition' of the Fragment," containing the sentence: "'Tradition' is what made it through war and the depredations of history."[16] Indeed if you neglect it, it will become "untraditional." If you fail to value and protect it, it may fall to unwanted pieces.

But let us not underestimate fragments. Let's make three. First choose a passage of your own writing to fragment (verb) that feels *too* whole, too tidy and tight.

Fragment 1: as if fragmented in/by anger, intense passion
Fragment 2: as if fragmented unintentionally, organically, a natural and unstoppable process of separation . . . like peanut butter separating . . . ice melting . . .
Fragment 3: as if fragmented lovingly, with tenderness, with a sense of *care* begetting precision

Share your fragments with a friend, and ask what they feel emanating from these shards relating to their genesis. Do they carry marks of their inciting emotion? Write a final fragmented poem that moves through anger, ambivalence, and tenderness, in any order, with these fragments.

____Primer

Caption your world for a day, and see how you change it or yourself. First explore Bertolt Brecht's *War Primer*,[17] an anti-war treatise for the ages in photos and captions. And when is war "hardly war?" Read Don Mee Choi's *Hardly War*,[18] an iconographic work of remembrance against empire.

For a full day, collect non-original (to you) imagery, from magazines to advertisements to photojournalism to media adverts. Where will you pull imagery from, and how will you engage it? What do you feel yourself being "primed" for through these images? When you've collected twenty-five, or whatever number you choose, write short lines of poetry to caption each. Tease, mock, praise, question, and insult these images, at your discretion. Speak to the people and things you see. Compile these into a small collection, titled "_____ Primer" if you wish.

Ghost(s) Of

Life and Death, the Shape of Grief, Selected Ghosts

Time

I read Diana Khoi Nguyen's *Ghost Of*,[1] a book concerned with life and death, grief and history, for the first time in 2020 in one immersive sitting, and then read it immediately again. I got stuck on a question: "*Why should we mourn?* / Isn't this the history we want / one in which we survive?"[2] The question appears in a poem titled "The Exodus," mapping both the literal and emotional terrain of a family's journey from "Saigon to Los Angeles, 1975–2015" (the poem's subtitle), as well as an adult speaker's return to Saigon which catalyzes the asking of the question. I was struck by the many ways this question can be asked, including from a generational *we* that has survived the horrors of the preceding generation but bear its psychic scars, and from the perspective of a single family who now *survives* a lost loved one. Both illuminate the unique pain of those who survive, grateful to live and achingly aware of the grief they will carry for the rest of their own lives. Survival is not so much a gift as a compromise, and mourning the way to accept it's been made. *Ghost Of* records grief itself, as a substance, a murk, a palpable environment where survivors live and in which secondary grief-events happen and/or find themselves trapped. On the details of the inciting events of grief, one of which is the suicide of a brother, Oliver, *Ghost Of* does not linger, meaning instead to grapple with what follows in grit and detail.

Oliver, both the presence and the absence of *Ghost Of*, by committing suicide, has escaped time, and has also altered the past forever with his act of cutting himself out of family photos from his childhood—images like the one in the figure, included in Khoi Nguyen's text.[3] Gone are the

Fig. 1. Family photo with cutout from *Ghost Of*

portals to the past, a world where Oliver lives and will continue to "live on," as the grieving like to say.

Though his act of cutting is undeniably a removal, the visual aftermath reads most like an act of replacement—an *additive* to the story of his family's life, rather than a subtractive event. His stark white absences solicit the eye. The preserved past is destroyed and replaced by one amended to reflect the present. The ghostly Oliver, heavy white, has always been there. His act eliminates his death as a hinge separating pre- and post-; there remains only Oliver's gone-ness in all times.

In 2023 I experienced, for the first time, an ambivalence about being alive, and the subsequent disorientation of realizing how strong this ambivalence was. It challenged my assumption that there was something inherently human about wanting passionately to live, and that my previous desire for life separated me in a meaningful way from other animal life on earth. Hadn't I believed it was a trait unique to our species to be actively *wanting* of life? And didn't that come with an obligation to continue to want life and oppose death? We depict the dead. We make imitations, replacements, doppelgängers, haunted amalgamations, and I felt certain that I wasn't ready to be remade in memorial. But when my ambivalence subsided, I felt sure that I had stained my life, or my right to life, with my deep and earnest ambivalence toward the only one I'd been given. And that stain at times seemed to move, to have shape or intention, and seemed in relationship to other stains from other times I'd turned my back on life, collapsing past, present, and future.

Violence

Not all absence is created equal, or neutral; some absence is not created at all. Sappho's fragments, provocative and thrilling in their "incompleteness," suggestively blank, are losses having almost nothing to do with Sappho, and everything to do with history. Time's winds and sands coauthor as they destroy. These processes of degradation themselves may be undiscerning, unintentional even, but their *access* to Sappho's papyrus over centuries is its own record of human neglect. Of Sappho's and Homer's military epics, Kazim Ali reminds us, "Both we had the care of. Yet we have much of Homer, and little of Sappho." What we call "tradition" in Ali's consideration of the uses and limits of fragmentation is in fact "what made it through war and the depredations of history. What was honored and carried through canon-makers like universities and governments." Traditions are "by definition imperial tools meant to circumscribe expression."[4] Shards and fragments of all kinds carry the traces of the violence of their making, including the violence of historical neglect, or, in Khoi Nguyen's depiction, the violence of their maker's exit from this world.

It's natural to not want to participate in violence. And yet that violence *creates*, and creates life even, is supremely natural. Animal and human sacrifice in antiquity (around the world) speak to our belief that crop, fertility, good health, and livelihood require payment, but is ultimately an equitable exchange. I offer a more recent example of consent and care: I ask my students if they would agree to participate together in an activity of controlled and restricted violence with me, in order to learn something about ourselves and our capacity for creation through destruction. It will involve cutting and slicing some words out of a piece of writing by somebody else in this class, I explain. But you will have that person's permission, freely given and freely recalled, if need be. You may at times feel a little bit uncomfortable, due to the destructive nature of your actions,

I say. You may also feel godlike. We'll learn much more about ourselves than anything about the original author.

Sometimes I encounter a word or image out in the world, on the subway or sidewalk in New York City, that feels not like a "whole" unto itself, but rather I have an oddly confident belief that it's the *shard* excised or freed from some other whole, elsewhere. I write this now from Iowa City, where I'm having this feeling about myself, temporarily sliced off from my real life in New York and deposited here for a semester of visiting teaching. Other times it's a word that carries the memory of its own lost sentence and immediately inspires a reconstructive effort in my head. Pieces of once-whole things are everywhere, broken umbrella stems, tires that sprang free from their axis, a child's shoe separated from the outfit lovingly assembled by her parents.

I attribute this thinking and sensation of "sentient shards" to *Ghost Of*'s powerful and serious consideration of the question: What happens to what is excised from us? In both the present and the past. In some cases it doesn't languish. It runs. If it's jagged and momentous enough it may return with its own unruly intention, to aim itself at the story we prefer to tell about our time with it. And if a swarm or school of shards assemble?[5] Khoi Nguyen shows us a visitation from the past(s) made literal, and not without antagonism on the part of grief's reanimated shards. We are *targeted*, and *sought*. To rest in peace is as much a wish we wish for ourselves (the living) as it is a blessing for the dead. Leave me be, we say. Let me rest in the shape of your absence in peace.

Also violent is the urge to fill in and remake the Oliver who has removed himself from both life and photograph, an urge both indulged and resisted by Khoi Nguyen's remade "Olivers" that move about the page with sentience. The Oliver cut from a photograph is reanimated with language, though still bound by the outlines of his earthly posture or silhouette. Importantly, as a remade figure, this Oliver doesn't fit grammatically *back* into the hole left behind in language—his new body only suggests an origin from the facing page, but he cannot reenter or complete any sentences with coherence. Oliver, once cut, is incompatible. There is no going back.

What does a shard of grief want for itself? What is it allowed to want? We give without much hesitation our pity and attention to the marred photos, "injured" as they seem to be, the nuclear family who was cut *from*.

Fig. 2. Swarm of shards from *Ghost Of*

But what of the cutter who freed himself? Is he gathered somewhere with the other Olivers—a field of selves?

Silence and Speech

Grief sounds like mania as often as it sounds like silence. When I was grieving my attachment to the future, which is how I came to understand that period of my life, I lost language, and felt as though I'd been sent back in time to live again as a child. I slept, and when I wasn't sleeping my bodily sensations were alien and alarming to me, so I cried until I could sleep again. This didn't endear me to life or its preservation, but because my life had become a respite from the burden of speech, I rested in silence. When I began to feel once again attached to life, I wanted to speak and write compulsively and to attach words to each little hook of my experience.

Gyotaku

Whether we leave a mark or an unsightly stain on life seems rarely, disconcertingly, up to us. Have I done enough? What will I leave behind? Departing the world without having imprinted on it seems, at times, intolerable. But to consider quantifying the marks made, monuments earned, and to take an honest inventory of them is a task soon overtaken by both the absurdity and joylessness of the task itself.

The tradition and art form of Gyotaku, Japanese fish printing, has utilitarian origins and was used to produce a documentary object for the purpose of cataloging the day's catch, recording details of size and species. A single mark, created by laying an entire inked fish onto paper, contained both profit record and aesthetic pleasure, neither function of the print needing prioritization over the other. Thus Gyotaku has a public-facing purpose, and is at least partially *for* public regard and information dissemination. *Ghost Of* is parsed by several moving poem Gyotakus, "prints" of grief that document and perform it for us simultaneously. Each spans two pages, the first a family photo distorted as if by vibration, with a fragment of language moving out from a cut in the photo,[6] or floating eerily inside the photograph like a fifth spectral figure.[7] On the Gyotaku's second page, this fragment *lives*, sentient and restless, printing itself repeatedly upon the page with a swarm-like frenzy, asserting both its existence and collectivity.

In the book's first Gyotaku, this fragment assembles and aims itself directly, and menacingly, toward the family photo it escaped from, the fragment's tip sharpened to a single letter, *t*.[8] Elsewhere a less sharpened fragment, released from a different family photo, assembles itself into a single enormous eel-like shape, the restless "elver" of *Ghost Of* associated with Oliver. The afterlife of this loss, Khoi Nguyen suggests, is hardly a blankness, rather a hyper-presence taking various forms, at times monstrous and with desires not beholden to the wishes of the living. Just as the tradition of the formal family photo is intended for public consumption, an advertisement for the nuclear family's strength, efficacy, and necessity, so does Oliver's loss enlarge and announce itself after breaking free from the confines of the frame.

As a documentary project, *Ghost Of* troubles easy categories of wanted and unwanted traces, and the complicated entitlement we may feel toward the legible grief of others. Is it right to want to leave without leaving a trace? Is it right to be dissatisfied by the memorabilia left behind for us by the dead? Oliver performs a creative act, modifying the photos of himself that exist in the world before leaving, amending them to reflect his passage out of body and time. His amendments are oriented, visually, toward a painful accuracy that cannot be undone.

A stain may be deeply associated with harm and hurt, but *Ghost Of*'s Gyotakus are far more interested in how the form's unimpeachable permanence signals other utopian possibilities that break the binary of absence and presence. In the book's final Gyotaku,[9] Oliver's absence from the family photo is most stark and extreme, even as the reader's eye is drawn to this same figure now composed of language (the sentient fragment Oliver) *alone* on the facing page. His face and body language turn fully away from the photo, and he nears the right-hand margin of the page, threatening to fully escape from view. But, behind him, a subtle new presence: a dense field of names, *oliver* and *elver* repeating in the faintest gray, so fully marking the page with their presence that it nearly goes unnoticed. Such traces seem to buoy the haste of the Oliver figure as he moves, a *residue* that coheres to become a new environment for the restless dead, moving toward where we cannot follow.

Fig. 3. Sharpened fragment from *Ghost Of*

Selected Ghosts

There are too many ghosts of my own haunting my readings of *Ghost Of*, and I allow them all. Some are traces of other texts, those ghosts that we call "influence." Others weigh upon me so heavily they form a fog through which I hope to at least occasionally see.

1. Sappho, her silence speaking louder than words, all that's been lost accusing us of its fate. In translator Anne Carson's evocative brackets, her losses are held open and one can hear the air rush and swirl into pockets, because "[e]ven though you are approaching Sappho in translation, that is no reason you should miss the drama of trying to read a papyrus torn in half or riddled with holes or smaller than a postage stamp—brackets imply a free space of imaginal adventure."[10] I swear I hear what fragments remain against a mighty whooshing, all that loss sounding itself at once.

As I root for narrative among the scattered brackets, occasionally turning up a word like some kind of truffle pig, I know I'm looking for no more than my own imagination there projecting itself onto her. I wish I could hold true time for every last loss—it might sound something like years of silence at a time, ruptured occasionally by a surviving word. Whatever sound time makes, if there is one audible to human ears, should be the sound sounded for each gap. One way is an exhale, another is a guttural human scream. One too delicate to be the sound of time, not violent enough, and the other too human.

2. The ghost in my language, English, is another language, Chinese. From middle school to high school I attempted to improve my Mandarin Chinese by attending Sunday afternoon Chinese lessons with other students from the Des Moines area. The classes were taught by my parents and their friends, and took place in the high school building where I otherwise attended class the rest of the week. After doing my American homework, there was Chinese homework remaining. I wrote the letters, stroke by stroke, in correct order, from left to right on the heavily gridded paper, meant to confine each stroke of each character to its correct quadrant. The constriction of the characters protects its meaning, each stroke in its place. Typically I copied each character ten times, and moved down one row to copy the next character ten times. Sometimes from among the ten versions of a character, because I was not talented at producing uniformity, I would choose my favorite, and designate it in my mind as the "real" one. It gave me a strange pleasure to "know" which character was the "real" one and that the other characters were impostors, though I didn't understand my own criteria. I rarely chose the most correctly written character. Sometimes I chose the one that looked the most squirrely and uncomfortable awkwardly splayed there inside its grid. If it appeared to me somehow sad and wrong, it felt real. This experience of trying to produce compliant characters was nothing like when my grandfather bought me a calligraphy set one summer and showed me how to grind the ink stick and properly wet the brush, before letting me draw imaginary characters all over the rice paper. I loved the inky "ssssssh" of the brush rounding a

curve, the strokes fading from saturated black to gray as each dip of the brush further diluted the inkwell. This was writing, though it produced no known words, and I understood that it need not.

3. This experience of calligraphy pings another—the work is Qiu Zhijie's *Writing the Orchid Pavilion Preface One Thousand Times*,[11] a performance piece where the artist copies over the famous "Orchid Pavilion Preface" on a single sheet of paper until it becomes illegibly saturated and blackened, a void so full of characters it appears empty. The "Orchid Pavilion Preface" is a calligraphy standard, often held up as a masterpiece of the art form as written by "father of calligraphy" Wang Xizhi. I can't deny that the piece speaks to the immigrant in me. The pious, culturally reverent selection of the "Orchid Pavilion Preface" that is copied so many times, or we could say made to reenact itself so many times, that it drowns in its own ink. The work is about "rejecting" or destroying the "Orchid Pavilion Preface" only if we believe that the ultimate purpose of the art form is executing a perfect reproduction. Qiu Zhijie's work speaks to me of duration as a function of reverence, memory, and incantation, and the flow-state of repetitive action. Importantly, this repetition does not produce anything, differentiating it from the repetitive action of an assembly line where one hundred pulls of a lever by a worker contributes to the completion of one hundred new iPhones, dishwashers, etc. The path of the artist's brush guided by memory, meaning it is guided by the past, makes nothing legible beyond its first try. It destroys its own product slowly over one thousand repetitions. I too wish to reenact the past, to trace and copy it, to feel my own muscles learn the strokes in their correct order, but the resulting product, the poem that explains itself and the memory of an event, disgusts me. It's too clear, too legible, so I must go over it again. And again. Ideally until I'm once again writing what doesn't exist, and can't exist, the imaginary characters that my grandfather once allowed me. What would that look like, as a poem? A thousand strokes that produced still nothing.
4. A writer who writes longing more vividly than anything held secure can be written, Mahmoud Darwish, one who writes the extreme nature of absence as it asserts itself, willful, irrepressible.

"The more you delve into your loneliness . . . the more longing takes you with motherly tenderness to its country, which is made of transparent, fragile fibers. Longing has a country, a family, and an exquisite taste in arranging wildflowers. It has a time chosen with divine care, a quiet mythical time in which figs ripen slowly and the gazelle sleeps next to the wolf in the imagination of a boy who never witnessed a massacre. Longing takes you around its country like a tour guide in heaven. It takes you to a mountain where you used to take refuge to wallow in wild plants until your pores soak up the smell of sage. Longing is smell."[12] Darwish speaks to us of those excised by violence, dispersed not by choice but by force, the fragments of a homeland that assemble in diaspora and exile, that *long* vividly together. "Longing has a country" when people do not, and denial of that loss is further injury. But Palestine is not a ghost, it does not *haunt*, it lives. And its presence grows.[13]

giovanni singleton's American Forms (Black Sisyphus; Don't Shoot)

Sisyphus, from Memory

He was a god, or he wasn't. He was a king, at least. He had some relation to both the gods on high, their glamour and power, and the lowly world of mortals. Of course you must imagine him with the stone, and it was a stone I'm sure, and he pushes it steeply and punishingly up the mountain. If it appears that he is preventing the stone from crushing him more than moving the stone, it's because he is. In this exercise he is avoiding death more than he is alive.

You must not ever imagine Sisyphus picking up the stone, heaving it onto his chest or broad back, because then you have imagined Atlas, the martyr. Sisyphus's fate is a result of his cleverness and his unwillingness to die not once but twice, and so Zeus devised to have him live forever and remain at his task. He stole something or somethings of great value, potentially not an object but a woman, or both, and did not show remorse. Why did he steal? For reasons other than altruism.

Why is Sisyphus's punishment so cruel? When does punishment transcend *gratuitous* and become almost *flamboyantly* sadistic? What makes it so?

You must first understand the anxious pride and delusion of Zeus, the punisher. His smallness touches all. You must picture him afraid, tempestuousness, paranoid, volatile, and fragile, meaning, he is exactly suited to devising punishment. To believing in it. He has a carceral spirit. For Sisyphus he must create a foremost temporal experience, so that Sisyphus feels the passage of time even as it will never run out; its passage teases its impossible cessation.

The punishment must also speak to Zeus's power by containing different emotional stages, a beginning, middle, and even end, which sets the cycle into motion again. Its relationship to narrative is part of its cruelty, as is the relationship of each portion of the punishment to hope. Where Sisyphus will suffer the most, and the least, where he will experience irrational optimism and where he will despair, has been considered. At the bottom of the mountain he must approach the boulder, drop his shoulders and head, place hands, and prepare to push. Though we see him there for the first time, we must remember that he has started there countless times before. Even so, there was a first time, and a second, and a third, and Sisyphus by design may have even experienced confidence bordering hubris in those early attempts. He may have believed that endlessness was only for those others too weak to put an end to their own suffering. This belief against even a god's will is the innocence and morality of children.

The journey's middle would be long, and full of suffering. But there must be a penultimate moment, when Sisyphus is able to see the top of the mountain, a place for the boulder to rest, the end of pain. Even the sanest sufferer would dare to hope, if only for that moment. That sensation of *progress* which culminates in a single engineered moment of disbelief in the permanence of one's own suffering is the most exquisite cruelty. It's what separates Sisyphus's punishment from eternal fire, eternal hunger, any number of relentless physical pains. The centerpiece of eternal hope is most cruel.

From memory, I can't recall how Sisyphus returns with his boulder (always I attribute the boulder to him, how it's *his* boulder, not Zeus's boulder) from the cruelest moment atop the mountain back down to the bottom to begin again. Perhaps he simply blinks and is returned to his task's beginning. But I imagine Sisyphus must watch the boulder roll back down the mountain, undoing his labors again, he must have to trudge after it and endure the long unchanging walk. And did Sisyphus ever refuse his task? Thus daring Zeus to confine him somewhere with simpler tortures, the easy pains of hot and cold, nothing compared to the cruelty of an unshakeable desire to *try*.

"Black Sisyphus—Take the High Road (a quadriptych: presently)"

Black Sisyphus, named, and in outline, in four panels, floats like a god against the starry cosmos winking in black and light. If I blink, Black Sisyphus lies on the asphalt, head crashing before his feet crash, rocks studding his body. He is the most high, and the most low at once.

How to close-read Black Sisyphus in whole? giovanni singleton suggests *don't*, see him instead just as he appears in this visual poem, from the collection *American Letters: Works on Paper* (2016), in four repeating movements, spring summer fall winter cycling forever, and try if you're able to allow him each movement before narrative urge sets in.

It begins with Black Sisyphus crashing; we meet him crashing, his trajectory clear. He is absence, in outline, hurtling towards a lower threshold slashed into the image as a black line. His right leg is bent, his right or left arm extended as if butterfly stroking against the asphalt. But with a blink, the eye resets. Black Sisyphus still swims, but cuts through the background elegantly, diving down below, bent towards the boundary line. Simultaneous to all, he is a chalk outline in a crime scene, the black jagged asphalt undeniable. There he lays, just as there he swims. But with a little imagination, the scene may change again, if we lay on our back looking up towards him as the most beautiful constellation, an eternal figure out of reach in the cosmos.

Another panel—Black Sisyphus aims his body upwards, he soars. He denies the ground, the boundary line below, he floats like a dazzling astronaut eager to breach the ceiling of the image. He rejects the frame. Or, he is splayed beneath us, and we are the god-head looking down. Have we done this? Have we allowed this? The imprint of his body that has been removed. And is this the same, or another? Black Sisyphus is name, or categorical fate? An unwilling brotherhood across centuries? The line beneath his gaze is now bordered above and below with a dotted line, shall we cut? Will he swim through it and come out the other side?

Now Black Sisyphus turns, his body does, indicated by three arrows turning counterclockwise. The pavement or the cosmos around him turns too, a celestial rotation, indicated similarly. As he turns he faces infinite directions, he is infinite possibility held in orbit. From above or below, there seems no force that can eject him from this cycle.

Black Sisyphus remains, in a final panel, laid out, inside an outline of America. Has America died too? Has America inscribed itself too as a recognizable entity in the stars? It encloses him, holds him womb-like or tomb-like and inert. This is a thoroughly American gestation, promised to live, gestated to die. Seen from above, Black Sisyphus is the largest man who has ever lived, a giant carved into the land, spanning coast to coast, able to touch all of his country at will. From below, Sisyphus and America immortalize each other in the unchanging stars.[1]

What road is this, and whose? "Take the High Road: Presently." It's difficult not to think of Michelle Obama's famous dictum that "when they go low, we go high" in 2016, speaking on bullying, but well-loved in the years since by liberals as shorthand for a thoroughly American rise-above-ism compatible with everything from racism to the gender pay gap. What exactly is the high road for Black Sisyphus, and for the country where he suffers? Taking the high road evokes what might once have been literal advice for Black motorists, drawn from publications like *The Negro Motorist Green Book*, a Jim Crow-era travel guide for Black roadtrippers on where to find establishments friendly to African Americans. Advice for this or that high or low road may indeed have been life-saving work. The phrase also hums with ghost phrases beneath the surface: "Be the bigger person," "Don't stoop to their level," "Don't give them the satisfaction," our American lexicon of "Just ignore it"-style racial harmony. That it is in fact just a matter of "roads" and which one you choose to take.

singleton asks us, movingly throughout, how high do you have to go when the roads lead to identical lands? When the boulders, institutionalized as law and enshrined as custom, remain?

Don't Shoot

singleton's "illustrated equation no. 1" depicts a black- and- white drawing of a handgun on the verso page, pointed right, towards a black- and-white drawing of a vintage hand-held camera at recto. The gun is labeled on its body as a SIG Sauer 40-caliber, the commonly issued police department weapon carried by officers, and the camera is a Super 8. The word "don't" appears beneath the handgun, and the word "shoot" appears beneath the camera.[2]

I can think of few images more iconically American than the gun and the camera, save for perhaps the American flag and the cross, both of which also appear elsewhere in *American Letters*. Placed in opposition to each other in this "illustrated equation," we're left to wonder if they are indeed meant to "equate" each other in some way (socially, morally, harmfully) or if their *aim* at one another undermines their equational form. The subtitle of the piece invites us, almost bemused in tone, to free associate: "something about a look . . . something about seeing . . ."[3]

What about a look, then? And what *about* seeing?

Americana, by which I use to mean that fantasy of America's white colonial settler power, has always loved guns and its own image. "Gun power" as a form, a social function, is rivaled only by media and gun *depiction*. From the cowboy westerns of manifest destiny expansionism to pulpy seemingly endless shows like *Law & Order*, the gun is truly ubiquitous, an object both constantly seen and threateningly concealed, desired and reviled. Consider as well the sheer number of hidden cameras (literal) and forms of surveillance (literal or panopticonic) most Americans come across daily, how poorly hidden their presence is in actuality and how we are coerced by necessity to ignore them. Consider the guns you know exist, the violence that can burst out in schools and public places, this paranoia paradoxically created by the image's concealment and assuaged by its invisibility. *Seeing* is indeed the concern on both sides of this illustrated equation, who sees through a scope and who is seen, who is "caught" on whose camera, the body- kind, or Hollywood kind.

The Americanness of these forms is their salesmanship, the fantasies of this country we readily purchase. Even though what they purport to offer and what they really beget are different, their supposed "face-off" in "illustrated equation no. 1" is performative and not truly adversarial, only visually so. Instead their orientation towards each other illustrates their exact co-creation of each other, an American Yin and Yang, complimentary necessities.

Real and imagined safety and violence animate both sides of the equation. For the citizen who "stands his ground," who imbues his weapon with both xenophobic paranoia and bootstrap-ism, safety and violence are one and the same. The ability to threaten to unleash violence at any time secures his selfhood. The adage that police don't keep anybody safe in America is false; police keep plenty of Americans and their ideologies safe, their mere existence and image safeguards a real (material) promise.

Gun-secured Americana is a white fantasy, one of competence and discretion, unperturbed by logics of (in)equity and its outcomes. singleton's visual equation permits the reading that surveillance (security camera, body camera) meaningfully "opposess" American guns, but of course we see repeatedly that abundant proof of violence does not itself end it. It is our fantasy that we project onto the camera, one of boundless oversight being equal to accountability.

A performance score follows this visual face-off in "illustrated equation no. 1," subtitled explicitly as an improvisation so that we understand this is a riff, a one-off, a spontaneous occurrence. I think of what Joyelle McSweeney, another poet of dazzling improvisational soundings, would call "sound as an event, a when, its frequencies made of repetitions. Sound it. Sound it again. Sound again and again."[4] This section of the poem is litany and list, as if all possible meanings and usages of "shoot" shouted themselves itself out. Soundings cascade:

snap shot
shoot a scene
shoot your mouth off
shoot footage
cell phone   body cam
shooter of the video
the one who shot the video
surveillance   surveillance
head shot

With "*shoot your mouth off*," a familiar and thoroughly American escalation is about to take place. As a surveilled subject, vulnerable to both gun and camera (as Black Sisyphus is also), a chain of events may soon lock into place when one shoots their mouth off at agents of the state. singleton continues,

United States of America, what's your emergency?
hot shot   big shot   good shot
Emergency, i seen him do it
camera shot
shooter   shoot him   shoot her
sir, turn around and get down on your knees[5]

singleton plays provocatively with sequence and association in this improvisation, allowing for the possibility of many realities at once. Is this artifice, a movie shoot? Or another police slaying? Who is being shot and in which way? A "good shot" for the "shooter" unsettles and confounds. Even here, the language of shooting[(s)] itself is careful to preserve plausible deniability. Best shots were taken, scenes were shot, someone shot the video, and someone was a hot shot. The latent violent acts only swirl, never cohere. The effect is of struggling to recreate a scene and identify fixed agents and subjects of violence, the connective narrative tissues having already decayed. The acts themselves simply swirl and float on, a story that can never be made straight.

For every child encouraged to "shoot for the stars" or "double shot" of espresso ordered, there is a command to shoot with deadly intent. Our language teems with germinating violence, and singleton's improvisation creates a heightened sensation of risk. After all, *chance*, in both improvisation and in police encounters, is a volatile factor. The poem's frenetic urgency and unpredictable chains of language rush us along, watching as a bystander would, towards a final quatrain rendition of Bob Marley's famous lyrics that command and elegize at once,

so get up stand up
stand up for your life
say get up stand up
stand up for your life . . .[6]

Music has the last word in singleton's American equation, worth saying not once but twice in this improvisation for life.

Three Transformations

Long Soldier, Atiya, and Alexander

I Recognize

That much is hidden in congressional or bureaucratic language, and all manner of language that keeps nations afloat, is a given. That it teems with subtext, that it is in fact language working very hard, covertly effortful, is perhaps less obvious. Incompetence, for people and texts, is a useful disguise. If we say it's banal, careless, meaningless, do we not also let it off the hook? The rhetorical engine of obfuscation never rests.

I'm thinking of many recent works of documentary poetry, where the insight and innovation of the poet so thoroughly transforms the source text that this remaking leaves us satisfied. Satisfaction is almost certainly the wrong word, but it does express something of the pleasure and activation that comes with reading an appropriation of what is often a violent, racist, and/or coercive document. Violent or evil speech is both condemned and highjacked to say the truth, to the reader's satisfaction. One phenomenon that illustrates this desire is what Rachel Stone called the "Trump-era boom in erasure poetry,"[1] an apparent surge in 2017 of writers and non-writers alike finding pleasure in making Trump, spewer and tweeter of prodigious violent speech, say what he would not willingly say using the technique of erasure. If Trump says he is not a philanderer, or a misogynist, or a liar, erasure can make him say that he is. It may be as simple as erasing his "not," to the pleasure of all who believe it to be true. As an act, it responds to the collective sense of anger, indignation, helplessness, and horror of watching Trump ascend to the presidency, providing catharsis by pulling truth from the very lie itself.

But sometimes there is much nuance (incriminatingly so) to be found in the original, unaltered text. Nuance that illuminates the specificities of its cravenness, that makes a defense of ignorance impossible. Such is the case with the source text used in Layli Long Soldier's poetry collection *Whereas*,[2] a poetic appropriation and subversion of the 2008 "Congressional Resolution of Apology to Native Peoples of the United States," signed by President Obama in 2009. No Native leaders were present at the signing, and the resolution itself was buried midway through a defense appropriations spending bill.[3] A text of such seemingly vigorous banality nearly succeeds in being written off as "meaningless," cowardly, yes, but nothing more. In fact what seems like not *trying* to apologize as a function of incompetence is actually a laboriously engineered text, like all legal texts that protect projects of empire must be. The enumerated "Resolution of Apology" section is worth reading in full, as it appears below:

> SECTION 1. RESOLUTION OF APOLOGY TO NATIVE PEOPLES OF THE UNITED STATES.
>
> (a) Acknowledgment And Apology.—The United States, acting through Congress—
>
> (1) recognizes the special legal and political relationship Indian tribes have with the United States and the solemn covenant with the land we share;
>
> (2) commends and honors Native Peoples for the thousands of years that they have stewarded and protected this land;
>
> (3) recognizes that there have been years of official depredations, ill-conceived policies, and the breaking of covenants by the Federal Government regarding Indian tribes;
>
> (4) apologizes on behalf of the people of the United States to all Native Peoples for the many instances of violence, maltreatment, and neglect inflicted on Native Peoples by citizens of the United States;
>
> (5) expresses its regret for the ramifications of former wrongs and its commitment to build on the positive relationships of the past and present to move toward a brighter future where all the people of this land live reconciled as brothers and sisters, and harmoniously steward and protect this land together;
>
> (6) urges the President to acknowledge the wrongs of the

United States against Indian tribes in the history of the United States in order to bring healing to this land; and

(7) commends the State governments that have begun reconciliation efforts with recognized Indian tribes located in their boundaries and encourages all State governments similarly to work toward reconciling relationships with Indian tribes within their boundaries.

(b) Disclaimer.—Nothing in this Joint Resolution—

(1) authorizes or supports any claim against the United States; or

(2) serves as a settlement of any claim against the United States.[4]

Even as "Resolution of Apology" purports to be neutral, steady in its remorse even, it grinningly gatekeeps "citizen" as a political and rhetorical category to the exclusion of Native Peoples. As it expresses, urges, commends, recognizes, and even "apologizes," it sinks deeper into its own patronizing passivity. Native Peoples have "stewarded and protected this land"[5] for thousands of years, cast into the role of a hired caretaker. It is clear that the subjectivities of Citizen of the United States and Native Peoples are mutually exclusive as the text deploys phrase after saccharine phrase: "positive relationships," "a brighter future," "brothers and sisters."[6] To move through this text as a reader is to allow its settler colonial ideology to speak for itself, and to hear it speak itself plain.

Long Soldier's seven "Resolution" poems from *Whereas*, enumerated to match the seven resolutions of the original document, are rich and varied for how they push beyond that initial (and important) documentary act of making the text betray itself. In Long Soldier's Resolution (1), which restricts itself to only the words that appear in the original Resolution (1) with the exception of the loaded insertion of "I" (this is true for all Resolution poems), two bolded phrases, "I recognize" and "the solemn," declare themselves against the gray text of the rest of the poem. The first word is the first person, importantly, an utterance of self, materializing where it did not exist before. The full poem reads,

(1)
I recognize

the special legal and
political relationship
Indian tribes have with
the United States and

the solemn

covenant with the land
we share.[7]

Imagine apologizing without an I, or a We, Long Soldier suggests, as the original apology does. Imagine apologizing instead through a complex triangulation of increasingly large and overlapping collectivities, named non-synonymously as the United States, the United States acting through Congress, the People of the United States, the President of the United States, the Citizens of the United States, and others. What is missing, certainly, that Long Soldier's appropriation adds, is a recognized selfhood, either as doer of harm or recipient, a place where responsibility and reparation can land. "I recognize . . . the solemn" floats above the rest of the poem as a phrase, hauntingly abstract—who or what is "the solemn"? A "solemn" so big or various, for such innumerable reasons, that it necessitates its own definite article. "The solemn" of this bloody history and its violent denial, indeed.

Resolution (2) begins again in this newly materialized first person, who commands a line alone atop the poem. To read the poem one way, priority may be given to the "intact" sentence from the original Resolution, which runs down the left-hand margin of the poem, neatly and tidily, "I / commend / and / honor / Native / Peoples / for / the / thousands / of / years / that / they / have / stewarded / and / protected."[8] Though no language has been added besides the first person "I," the statement of commendation now rings sincere, true, even sentimental. The patronizing tone is gone. It would appear, Long Soldier shows us, that the violence and injury was not inherent to the language, it was located fully in the speaker. In this reading, the rest of the poem is thrillingly wild by contrast to the neatness of the left-hand margin—repetitions of "this land" fill the field of the page, without recognizable order or governance, unpruned and unparceled, suggestive of endlessness and sprawl, free and erratic. "This land" is boundless, scattered, insistent, it disorients the eye as all untouched spaces do, and it speaks repeatedly (literally) for and of itself.

Another reading of these repetitions is more fractious, equally evocative, and stages an antagonism between the sentence patronizingly commending Native Peoples and the phrase "this land," which disrupts and disturbs each word of the sentence. "This land" becomes protest, inconvenience, and threat—a thorn in the side of the sentence's desire to complete itself. "This land" echoes and returns again and again, unpredictable and fragmented without discernible pattern, but assertive of itself between each word:

I
commend this land
and this land
honor this land
Native this land[9]

The fixation on "this land" is simultaneously ours, the poem's, and the congressional language's, enacted obsessively to discomfiting effect. It has always been about "this land," naming it and parceling it and owning it, or protecting it and cohabitating with it, depending again on which subjectivity is speaking. As Long Soldier shows again, the violence is not always inherent in the language. Even an insistence on "this land" need not do harm, and is capable of transmitting care.

And what to make of the small but prominent square amid all this land repeating itself?

honor this land
Native □ this land
Peoples this land
for this land
the this land
thousands this land

As placed it draws the eye, its perfect uniformity at odds with the organic scatter[10] of this land—perhaps it has more in common with the perfectly portioned sentence of commendation running down the poem's left margin. Visually alien and sterile, approximating that most man-made form: the border. Four together to make an enclosure, a within and without, an infrastructure of domination upon "this land." If a reader were to remember an earlier appearance of this shape, in a poem entitled "Ȟe Sápa," they might recall the words that make up the four not-yet-enclosed walls of that larger square: "This is how you see me the space in which to place me / The space in me you see is this place / To see this space see how you place me in you / This is how to place you in the place in which to see."[11] On the land or in the mind, the enclosure is a blight, an abomination.

Resolution (3) returns a third time, with intensity, to Long Soldier's insistent first person, and again to its powerful *recognition*, a recognition of specificity and accusation that transforms that initially meaningless verb:

(3)

I

recognize

that[1]

official[2]

ill-[3]

breaking of[4]

the[5]

Indian[6]

This first person recognizes and bestows the appropriate kind of "recognition" squarely upon "that / official / ill- / breaking of / the / Indian."[12] "Official ill-breaking" rings out not so much as a forced confession by the text, but as a succinct and damning charge via recognition of crimes. The purview of the poet here is to *recognize* and name both violence and its sanctioned nature, official and never accidental as it has always been.

As in much of Long Soldier's work, readers also have a choice (and indeed must do much choosing) in these Resolution poems. In Resolution (3) this takes the form of six footnotes, attached to each word after "I / recognize." Footnotes, it seems, are very personal, and not coincidentally associated with "scholarly writing" of the sort that produces official histories and agreed-upon versions of events. Serious readers have serious feelings about their role on the page, the correct way to read (or delay reading) them, and to what extent they should disrupt (many wouldn't use that word) the linearity of a reader's experience. Some readers see footnotes as essentially bad feng shui, forcing an awkward physical arrangement between primary and secondary language, and forcing a repetitive back-and-forth movement that is decidedly bad flow. Depending how you read footnotes and if you do, and what authority you lend them, you will either encounter Long Soldier's newly constructed statement of recognition (above), or, you will dutifully move back and forth between poem and footnote to succeed in reconstructing the original congressional language: *I recognize that there have been years of official depredations, ill-conceived policies, and the breaking of covenants by the Federal Government regarding Indian tribes.*[13] Of course with one recurring exception: Long Soldier's change in subjectivity such that *I* is recognizing now. The language may remain unchanged and unsoftened, but *I* is atop this recognition for good.

As for what all this participation on our part implies, I'm suspicious of generalized "complicity" readings that only seem to prematurely dead-end our thinking around the reader-writer relationship. Certainly contact with the American colonial project has heaped complicities upon us all, but the buzzword-ificiation of "complicity" threatens to render every soul found "complicit" immediately politically inert, disqualified from future solidarities, slotted into yet another devastatingly American binary of innocent and complicit. The impulse to spend long swaths of time reflecting upon one's American complicity at the expense of delaying one's agency as a political actor should be suspect, as surely the American project would prefer for us to introspect ourselves to death. If ever I felt a poem entreating me to cut through the noise of political speech and political inertia to *recognize* and thus stand a chance of moving past recognition, it is this one.

I'm Hungry

In 2015, I came across Amber Atiya's poem "New York State Office of Temporary and Disability Assistance SSI/Food Stamp Benefits Application," published on the website *Literary Hub*.[14] My poetry world was still very small then. I was fresh out of formal studenthood, by which I mean the lucky years where someone older and wiser than me would tell me what to read, push me to actually read it, tell me that my poems and my forms were tired and in need of air, that my little lyric epiphanies were (yes) getting predictable. I was at the beginning of an important disillusionment *with* the lyric, with lyricism and its both noble and insufferable urge to adorn, smooth, and *sing*. Formal experimentation and energy intimidated me as a young poet, as it intimidates many more young poets today, and our intimidation across time and place bonds us in a way that makes me feel tender. It was a good fear, one that urges onward.

Thus why I was so importantly jarred and enchanted by Atiya's poem's total disinterest in the comforting ways of the lyric, and rightly so, as this poem is hungry, is *authored* by "i'm hungry," is signed "i'm hungry." Atiya's poem uses the form named in its title, the New York State Office of Temporary and Disability Food Stamps SSI Benefits application, to create a performance script that stages an interaction rooted in callousness, cruelty. The application form asks and probes, while the hungry speaker answers again and again while insisting on their own hunger:

> **Name** i'm hungry
> **SS #** what this iz?
> **Address** southside a union square park
> **Phone#** no
> **Are you/have you ever been a drug abuser?** sometimez to stop the hunger

Have you ever been convicted of a felony? yea but i only stole cuz i wuz hungry

* *Felony crime are serious crimes that include burglary and murder. Felons lose many of their civil rights: the right to run for office, join the military, and vote can be taken away. Prospective employers have the right to inquire about any felony convictions. Many insurance companies will not insure convicted felons making it difficult for felons to find work.*[15]

Throughout, italicized asides are deployed in a threatening manner under the thin guise of being informative, such as the passage above about felony crimes, itself only a small part of what The Friend (in introducing Atiya's poem for *Literary Hub*) correctly described as the "Kafka-like bureaucracy that somehow must manage, categorize, and interrogate human suffering through endless paperwork."[16] To call the labyrinth of suffering "red tape," as we sometimes do, risks implying that the dysfunction is a naturally occurring phenomenon that is not designed or enforced with any intention. As the poem goes on, Atiya's speaker's hunger becomes their totalizing identity and desire, the neutralization of hunger being naturally the only goal of the hungry. When asked, do you have "Chronic Heart Failure," the speaker replies "from hunger?" and checks the box. Several questions down the form are further cruel and direct while the speaker continues to affirm their hunger:

Are you hungry? i'm hungry

Do you need food stamp benefits rights away? i'm very hungry[17]

Readers watch as the poem's speaker navigates one of this country's great shames, the barriers to food, housing, healthcare, and education, all the while insisting on their own humanity as a person who hungers. The form shames itself with each subsequent question and each next word that is not food, not relief from hunger.

Atiya's poem is staging that most American encounter, between arbitrary weaponized credentialization and human suffering. The poem itself is experiential, as a script, giving readers the lines to answer the form, putting our speech through the interaction without purporting to teach or describe. One might say that hunger supersedes all other urges, be they lyric, descriptive, narrative, or sensory. What is all this language doing when one is hungry? Atiya asks: How can it even justify its own proliferation down the page? If repetition emphasizes, then this repetition of inquiry emphasizes its own cruelty powerfully. By contrast, Atiya's speaker as scripted in this interaction draws out the monstrosity of her inquisitor by somehow (even through hunger) brimming with a playful dynamism. An aliveness that insists. Her responses are by turns defiant, amused, ironic, scathing, and seemingly aware of the presence of an audience for which to perform, even with a little wink at times. When asked, "**Are you an illegal alien?**" by the application form, the poem's speaker responds by crossing out "illegal alien" and writing in the word "immigrant," and adding "i ain't from across no outta space borderz."[18] This moment is a transgression, where the speaker crosses the threshold of authority to correct and reprimand the inquisitor, to cheekily reply to them: aliens . . . like from outer space?

Atiya's poem is not interested in breaking apart the original and remaking it in any new image. Its punishment, it seems, is to be itself. You might call this preservation of evidence. Anecdotally, I have never shared this poem with students or readers where somebody doesn't ask what the whole group seems to be thinking: Is this application form real? The litmus test function and conceptual heft of Atiya's poem is remarkable. Readers' certainty about how much is "real" reveals much about their own positionally and contact with this country's mechanisms for aid. Readers who have had little contact with food assistance or public assistance benefits are sure, often *very* sure, that the form is not the real form given to food assistance applicants, citing the clearly irrelevant and absurd nature of some of the questions. Readers who have themselves relied on food assistance or have helped a loved one navigate the program are far less sure that it's *not* real, seemingly unbelievable as it may be, given past experiences of such surreal unhelpfulness and inscrutability as to give them pause.

Atiya's poem challenges the very optimism that we wish to have about the country we live in, asking us if we're sure that this nation is above asking food assistance applicants "Are you muslim" or "Please solve the following equation: / 3f(x) + 5xf(x) = 11 / (*Your ability to solve this equation will greatly / impact your eligibility for SSI/Food Stamps*)"[19]

That this form is assumptive is an understatement, and yet bears repeating, harmfully full as it is of such outsized beliefs about who the hungry are, who they should be, and how they've failed to deserve food by virtue of health, job status, race, immigration status, and more. The poem's speaker convincingly performs her role as exactly who she is meant to be, an amalgamation of qualities that pre-certify her as Undeserving in the eyes of the state: sick, unhoused, unemployed, mentally ill, racialized suspiciously, though never lacking a sense of humor. When asked about cancer status, the speaker responds, "i still got my left titty and it / iz hungry," and when asked "please list the names of your / multiple identities" (for Dissociative Identity Disorder) she offers "florence, mary & diana."[20] Each time I read this poem, it strikes me powerfully that any indignity and rage that I feel is a feeling produced inside of me and projected onto the speaker of the poem, who herself only expresses, repeatedly, hunger and occasional humor. To locate my anger is to see that it is made possible by my absence of hunger, my ability to exist outside of that identity, and my understanding of the situational cruelty that the poem is enacting as a performance text. To be hungry, Atiya reminds us, is to *be* hungry. And the cruelty of our systems demands more.

Please Eat

"Please Eat" is the title of a long list poem by Sarah Jean Alexander (2016)[21] composed entirely of daily text messages sent to the author over the course of a year by her mother, in Korean, which Alexander then translated into English using Google Translate. It's also, as a phrase, that most familiar, comforting, and equally controlling entreaty from many Asian and immigrant parents to their children, adult or otherwise. Please eat means I love you, and can also mean I'm upset with you, it can be a form of punishment or congratulations. It is, despite the "please," fairly nonnegotiable in most contexts. For Alexander, it's the first of a year of text messages that her mother chooses to send, thus it is the opening line of the poem, followed by other daily phrases (what you might call "useful phrases") such as greetings, days of the week, and months of the year. The poem begins

> Please eat
> Come on in

Good morning
Take your strength?
Sit
Did you sleep well?
What kind of job do parents have?
What day is it today?
Mom loves our daughter a lot.
How many brothers are there?
Today is Sunday
Mom hates tattoos too much.
Today is very busy Day
Today is Wednesday . . . It's pretty in black.
Today is Thursday - come rain
Today is Friday - Let's go to lunch
Today is Saturday - Where did you come from?
Today is Sunday - Let's go play
Today is Monday - the weather is getting colder
Today is Tuesday - Do not
January - Wipe your hands
February - Today is Thanksgiving
March - we go on a journey
April - will travel to other countries
May - be careful!
June - the weather was very hot.
July - this is very beautiful here
August - How are you?
September - the leaves are pretty.
October - Did you learn Korean language a lot?
November - I go home today
December - Today is a Christmas mystery.
Do you like to live in New York?[22]

Readers soon understand these texts, despite being arranged now as a poem, to have instructive intent, and do not represent an ongoing "real" conversation between mother and daughter. The phrases are foundational knowledge for a new language learner, phrases to establish time and place, weather, numbers, and how to make nice small talk with others. The mother sends texts to instruct; the daughter, theoretically, receives and studies. But some days a sense of the world outside this exercise intrudes, including the existing tensions between mother and daughter participating in this instructive conceit. One day's text reads, "Mom hates tattoos too much."[23] Does the daughter have tattoos? Or did her mother see a tattoo that upset her sensibilities or beliefs? Is this irritation, or worse, admonishment? The pinprick discontent of the text enters the poem, both mysterious and suggestive, betraying more than a little porousness between a mother's instinct to instruct and her desire to air grievances.

Throughout, details emerge about this family, and the intense concerns of a mother who is missing her youngest daughter, who dotes upon her when she visits from New York City, and who thinks about her often. Texts of affirmation are abundant: "Mom wants to see Sarah a lot," "You are as beautiful as an angel."[24] There are also trips to the doctor, to Boston, to see various other family members, remarks about exercising and health, and about going to church. On this topic the author's mother is quietly relentless, beseeching her daughter "to pray to God every day," "Read the bible," "It is Sunday. Go to Church," "Join a church today," and advising that "Even though a man plans his way with his heart, he who guides the way is Jehovah."[25] As the suggestions to find a relationship with God accumulate in the poem, readers understand unambiguously that this is repetition as complaint, and something that the author's mother wants deeply for her youngest daughter. In and among these suggestions are passages animated by latent fear, a vague sense of barely keeping poor health and insidious unknowns at bay, further evidence of the necessity of faith. One period of just over three weeks bookended by calls to faith reads:

> Pray everyday.
> Did you have a hard time working?
> Our youngest daughter, meet a good man, and get married.
> Spring is here.
> The flowers are very bloody.
> What plan do you have today?
> It is the day when Mom and Dad come home.
> I'm comfortable sleeping in my bed.

Monday is the beginning of another week.
I like the view.
I love Sarah a lot.
Be careful wherever you go.
There are a lot of scary things going on.
The sky is very clean.
My body is not good, but I recommend doing a little exercise.
Sarah how are allergic reactions?
Happy Easter!
How is your body today?
I hope to have a good day.
The pool was quiet today.
The wind is blowing a lot.
I think my neck muscles are wrong.
I could not sleep how much the wind blew last night.
Read the Bible.[26]

As these months go on, and the poem departs from instructive intention, prescriptive and didactic advice begin to take its place, along with more fear, commands to piety, and questions about health and happiness. This daughter will be unlikely to need the phrase herself "Mom worries, please contact me often" or "I am really sorry that I was hard on my daughter yesterday"[27] in Korean. Instead these ring of familial specificity, connected to experiences of conflict and reunion, arguably one and the same. What emotes here, and what has brought me back to read "Please Eat" dozens of times, is the tenderness with which the silent recipient daughter and her verbose mother are both trying to reach each other over the course of the year. None of this is contained in a single pithy line. The lyric has nothing to do with it, you might say, though the imagery and poeticism of some of the lines are beautiful. "The flowers are very bloody," the mother writes one day, and "My eyes are in a storm." "I'm going to go to the mountain and play with the mountain today."[28] To decide that these poeticisms belong to Google Translate and were not originally intended to be surreal images of nature is to cut off some of the surprising potential of how we imagine this Korean mother's relationship to language. Is it possible, writing to her daughter who is a poet, that she might experiment some? That she might try to overcome the distance between with poetry?

Teaching is the first parental act, but then we are left to ourselves as two people, child and parent, to figure out the rest. We might commune through imitation, Alexander suggests, both trying out the other's language(s) in more ways than one. "Please Eat" is structurally an effort to build a relationship of dailiness with the Korean language on one end, and a promise to show up in the life of one's adult child on the other end. The resulting poem is a third language, something more than an English transcript of Korean text messages, a place where two people can meet. Yet in the blink of a reader's eye, a year has passed. The completion of this archive is somehow as sorrowful as it is filled with a sense of achievement, acknowledged by the mother in the poem's last two lines: "Do you know what today is? / It was the day I started sending Korean words to my daughter."[29]

The Destruction of the Earth Is the Destruction of All Childhoods

A Memory in Second Person of a Discussion of Inger Christensen's *Alphabet*

You remembered to bring the book, the hard copy, so that when you espouse the value of hard copies you won't seem ridiculous. You then say something about how in order to read in a form-forward way, we should spend some time with whatever form a poem takes and let ourselves into the work through that door. This is when you take out the stock image of the "golden ratio" that you've made copies of, and pass them out sheepishly. You feel self-conscious and clarify that this is helpful for those who are visual learners, like yourself. It's math, you say, it's a visual representation of the Fibonacci sequence, where each number is the previous two numbers added together, i.e., 0, 1, 1, 2, 3, 5, etc. It gives us this shape that you're looking at, you say, and trace the outlines of the curve—it also gives *Alphabet* its form. Even now, in front of everyone, you'll smile at how beautiful it is, how elegant, the curve opening outward from a central point, growing exponentially, shell-like, found all over in nature.

You find yourself asking the group: is it pleasing to you? You show some photos of objects in the world that supposedly illustrate this ubiquitous ratio, among them cauliflower, the shape of the human ear, various flora and fauna. You ask the group if it soothes, tames? Or does it unsettle, explode? Surely it does both, someone will say, the swirl and gentle rise of it, the pleasing proportions that grow at a predictable pace. When we say predictable, do we mean controllable? You can imagine, looking at it now, the moment such exponential growth grows past that threshold of control, the explosion, the moment it becomes entirely uncontainable fission, that which annihilates and engulfs.

But first, you say, let's try a small version of a Fibonacci poem, to put our bodies through the physical experience of generating this growth. Let's write a poem where each line has this many number of words:

0
1
1
2
3
5
8
13
21
34

You feel excited to try this writing with them, and to experience the sensation of elongation and propulsion, to be unsettled by it. You think to yourself and then say aloud that there might be a moment where the growth becomes fear, when it intimidates and grows out of your hands. In life, you ask, when have you experienced restriction that doesn't seem to constrict the outcome at all? A constriction that drives and exerts its will? What does growth like this feel like? You consider together all the associations of New Growth, the effort to keep things growing at the cost of so many living things dying. The Degrowth Movement,[1] after all, is a movement to save all that has to die in order for New Growth in a capitalist system to continue ad infinitum. You'll also think, oddly, about finding growths on your human body, the alarm and the confusion, knowing that as forever chemicals accumulate in the service of such New Growth there are unknowable cancers and malignancies growing similarly unchecked.

Here, a pause, a jump in time, it is no longer 2021, it is 2024, almost 2025, and you will soon introduce Inger Christensen's *Alphabet* (trans. Susanna Nied)[2] again to your beloved students. You are thinking about all the talk of the Covid-19 pandemic "in the rearview" while it spikes all around you. Premature historicizing, like closing your eyes while still driving. You are also thinking of Hannah Cooper-Smithson writing of the canonization (already, astoundingly) of what we might understand to be Covid-19 literature, a "pandemic poetics," the same way that Christensen's *Alphabet* refracts the nuclear anxiety present in much literature of the cold war.[3] You hadn't yet read Cooper-Smithson's piece the last time you revisited *Alphabet*, and you make a mental note to share it with students while reminding them that what we (all of us) write now will shed light in the future on our moment. You wish to return to the beginning of *Alphabet* and read it, that bright and foreboding sorrowful beginning, "apricot trees exist, apricot trees exist." Each time you attempt to hear it simply you are only able to hear the worry in it, the precarity of all living things and the love for them that necessitates the repetition. If only apricots trees could exist more. Christensen writes,

> 1
> apricot trees exist, apricot trees exist
>
> 2
> bracken exists; and blackberries, blackberries;
> bromine exists; and hydrogen, hydrogen
>
> 3
> cicadas exist; chicory, chromium
> citrus trees; cicadas exist;
> cicadas, cedars, cypresses, the cerebellum
>
> 4
> doves exist, dreamers, and dolls;
> killers exist, and doves, and doves;
> haze, dioxin, and days; days
> exist, days and death; and poems
> exist; poems, days, death[4]

Bracken, blackberries, bromine, hydrogen, the great alphabetical inventory of things has begun. Cicadas, chicory, chromium, citrus trees, all is named and thus comes into the poem, which for a reader at the moment of reading is the world. Before the naming: nothing. This is the beautiful knot of *Alphabet*, one of many: that doves existed in the world before they were named doves, which is to say before they needed a name, before we looked upon them, and even after us they have no need of naming to exist. But once we *have* named the world, something follows, and the existence of such things (doves, days, trees) ceases to be guaranteed. When we've made known the living things, and wanted them, we risk them. Even now, you think, how could naming be an act of preservation? Aren't all things placed alphabetically into the bullseye of annihilation? To name the trees and the fruit, is it not to place them in harm's way, in our gaze? *Alphabet* asks us to look, even as we know that our human interest has only ever yielded catastrophe. It is the most destructive gaze that exists.

But of course, naming does risk and preserve at once. Such growth contains its own seed of destruction, and yet relies on itself to create its own living memory. As names beget names, as they always have since Genesis and the naming of sons, naming has also begot destruction as sons and creations turn on their fathers. *Alphabet* is life and death multiplying at once.

But. Back to then.

It's an evergreen question you ask about *Alphabet*, which is also about all the world: How does a threat, a risk, catastrophe, enter? Impossible not to think of all the risk and catastrophe there is to think of, that has entered the world incontrovertibly, and now you'll speak this in front of readers who themselves entered the world amid seemingly endless roiling catastrophes. A young reader reads in the age of climate collapse, not as abstraction but lived reality, of poisoned water, of wildfires, of critical infrastructure no longer able to handle the rising temperatures, of mass gun violence, of apparently unforgivable student debt. These crises tend existential, and like Cooper-Smithson wrote about Covid-19, each has "brought the connectedness of the globe and the collective identity of our species to light in a way that echoes the threat of species death from nuclear technologies."[5] "Killers exist"[6] indeed, as Christensen writes, and you are thinking this in a nation legislated by them, in a period of openly genocidal activity.

In the world of *Alphabet*, catastrophe enters as it often does, in that most banal way, with a word, an utterance that can't be undone. Death exists and is accounted for, just as poems are, and the existence of hydrogen hangs over the poem, having entered it so early. In Christensen's genesis story, hydrogen's arrival also brashly violates the formal strictures of this alphabetical world, as stanza A passes alphabetically to stanza B, hydrogen enters without permission, before its determined time. Similarly killers, haze, and poems, will each violate the alphabetical order and assert themselves prematurely into this inventory of the world, unruly. In all these utterances, a sense of inevitability: that if all must be named (and it must), it must *all* be named, even dangerous proximities, even as "the products of fission exist; / errors exist, instrumental, systemic, / random"[7]

If *Alphabet* is a vision of pristine nature, it itself already contains every ingredient for life, death, accident, illness, destruction, and annihilation. Atom bombs, it seems, will eventually exist, and the shock of their arrival jarringly arrests Christensen's form:

> Atom bombs exist
>
> Hiroshima, Nagasaki
>
> Hiroshima, August
> 6th, 1945
>
> Nagasaki, August
> 9th, 1945
>
> 140,000 dead and
> Wounded in Hiroshima
>
> Some 60,000 dead and
> Wounded in Nagasaki
> . . . .
> The children of the wounded
> Stillborn, dying

Many, forever a
Few, at last the
Last: I stand in

My kitchen peeling
Potatoes; the tap
Runs, almost
Drowning out the
Children in the yard;[8]

Though you have read this passage many times, you will never not shiver facing this pronouncement of existence, which of course is a pronouncement of history, a memory, no longer a premonition. As the *name* goes off in language, you imagine the splitting of atoms exponentially into death. It pauses inventory; it pauses all. It demands enumeration, numbers and dates, and it necessitates the first appearance in this world of "I," that lyric avatar withheld (held back? Or reluctant?) until now, heralded by the atomic bomb's existence.

And who is this I? Human, small, standing in the kitchen peeling potatoes, able to hear the children shouting over the birds who shout over the wind, the leaves drowning out the sky and the light. You will think to yourself how dark, and correct, this order of things, this human invention bringing forth the first human presence in this world. Singularly "I" is a witness, a bard to tell of it. But "I" is reliably destructive as a species.

Here in the present of 2024, you read Sharon Lerner's deeply reported piece on the prevalence, beyond imagination, of synthetic fluorochemicals, specifically PFAS (a categorical name for forever chemicals), and one specific chemical created by the 3M Corporation named PFOS (short for perfluorooctanesulfonic acid) in our world. And our world, it is important to specify, includes our blood. It is nearly impossible today to find a living human being on earth, save for someone who might have lived their entire life in the remotest parts of the globe, who does not have forever chemicals in their blood. You remind yourself that it's no longer forever chemicals "in" our hair, or "on" our skin and food, forever chemicals *are* our hair, nails, skin, blood. You think about this when you put in your contact lenses in the morning, the slim disk of plastic that floats painlessly and perfectly on your eyeballs during the day thanks in part to the wetting properties of PFAS, and not unlike PFOA, another forever chemical that is used to make Teflon non-stick. 3M are also notably the inventors of Post-it notes, Scotch tape, and Scotchgard for fabrics.[9]

The images you see repeatedly in your mind are the viral photos[10] from 2009 of dead albatross chicks with their stomachs full of plastics in bright cheerful colors. Desiccated and sunk into the grayish sand, the albatrosses' colorless bodies morbidly frame the plastic detritus, smooth and turquoise, pink, orange, bright red. As filmmaker and environmentalist Jo Ruxton commented, the photos seemed to resonate with people because the plastic objects are still recognizably *our* things; we relate when "[we] see things that we actually use, that have passed through [our] hands."[11] Toothbrush covers, plastic caps, floss, bits of packaging, most pieces still identifiable. It's almost darkly quaint now, you think, the idea that body and pollutant (albatross and plastic) though mixed up for a while, are still separate, can still be "cleaned," objects removed from the sickened body, the sickened ocean. Fluorochemicals render degrees of "pollution," that beloved word of the nineties environmental movement, obsolete. We are less "polluted" these days than invaded, overtaken, colonized by. Unlike a tumor (New Growth), a search-and-destroy approach is impossible; excision is a fantasy for the past. You think about what an inventory or elegy or premonition for our moment might be, faced with the understanding that these synthetic chemicals are literally our inheritance, PFOS passed down from mother to child. Giving birth, it's suspected, based on testing of female rats, is the only time in a living adult's life where the accumulated levels of PFOS in her body will decline—passed on to her baby.[12] How do the specific contours of this surreal catastrophe compel us, its heirs, to write?

Rereading *Alphabet* is to reexperience a barrage of "exists" swirling all around you, to give yourself up to that word repeating. You realize of course that you're not only experiencing a repetition but an insistence of, an urging, an incantation. You think of Gertrude Stein on the matter:

> A thing that seems to be exactly the same thing may seem to be a repetition but is it . . . Is there repetition or is there insistence. I am inclined to believe there is no such thing as repetition. And really how can there be . . . Expressing anything there can be no repetition because the essence of that expression is insistence, and if you insist you must each time use emphasis and if you use emphasis it is not possible while anybody is alive that they should use exactly the same emphasis.[13]

You ask your fellow readers if they agree with this, philosophically or otherwise, however they like: Is it possible to repeat? Can repetition *only* amplify, emphasize? It becomes an interesting activity, trying together to think of a time that "repeating oneself" was emotionally neutral. In your family, it was always slightly threatening, and maybe this is common but you're not sure. For your parents it was certainly important, as you were made to understand that the essence of a parent was to repeat-as-escalation, an emphasis of a different sort. Christensen's escalation is rooted in optimism, as if this repetition really could save all the living things of the world. Didn't Noah do this too in the Old Testament? A repetition of each animal, to save them all.

You love the tenderness and arrogance of the poet, charging herself with the naming of all things, to give the world order with one's love. You're thinking about how this poem creates and elegizes at once, to insist on each thing at least once before it disappears. The poet with all her foresight can't stop the world by naming it, but she does confer more than just awe and affirmation. Christensen *names* and also names *names*, placing blame where it's due as *Alphabet* becomes increasingly apocalyptic. The Teller Group, the Sakharov Group, the British, French, Chinese, and their colonial crimes enrage the earth itself, "the waves of the / Pacific rag[ing] in fury."[14] As Brecht famously reminded, there are no worlds where abstract malevolent forces periodically enact their will: "evil has an address. It has a telephone number."[15] To believe that evil deeds perform themselves is a missed opportunity to un-obscure the face of its doer. In this future, Christensen tells us, it would be a gift to be granted one's "plea to die / as people used to die / one day in ordinary // weather, whether you / know you are dying / or know nothing, maybe // a day when as usual you have / forgotten you must die, a breezy day in / November maybe."[16]

Another great namer of names, the poet Diane di Prima, in her poem "Revolutionary Letter #15," urging radical political struggle against institutions and even more radical solidarity, writes,

> When you seize Columbia, when you
> seize Paris, take
> the media, tell the people what you're doing
> what you're up to and why and how you mean
> to do it, how they can help.[17]

Tell the people what you do, if you're not ashamed to be doing it, and if you see that which should be ashamed to be done, tell it too, and let the doers be recognized alongside their deeds. Speech acts and evil acts can still oppose each other in this world (and our world too, you hope).

The stanzas before *Alphabet*'s prematurely final section, section N (when "nuclear" would appear, obliterating all), finds the poem's "I" insisting urgently on body and writing, a catalog of the flesh that houses the self:

> I write like the beating
> heart writes
> the hands the feet
> the skin the lips
> the sex their whisper
>
> I write like the beating
> heart writes
> the muscles the lungs
> the face the brain
> the nerves their sound
>
> I write like the beating
> heart writes
> the blood the cells
> the visions the tears
> the tongue their cry[18]

Reading this late passage of Christensen's elegy for the future as only despairing or containing some premonition of impending destruction is to miss the profound optimism it takes to insist on a vision against the one that seems inevitable. Around the country this year (it is 2024) the movements for Palestine and the campus encampments to divest from death have shown us how to name names, where to push with others once the names have been read, and how to alchemize rage into hope by naming exactly what it is that's happening to the world you love. You hesitate to call *Alphabet* a dirge only because it's not funerary, per se, at least not without dreams of resurrection, but it does save the lament for this world's most stinging loss for the end of the poem: not the loss of the children, who may yet survive, but the children's childhoods. In the apocalyptic *after* of section N,

a group of children seeks shelter in a cave
mutely observed only by a hare

as if they were children in childhood's
fairy-tales they hear the wind tell

of the burned-off fields
but they are no children

no one carries them any more[19]

The destruction of the earth is the destruction of all childhoods, you will think while looking at your students, even your own childhood which you have already finished living but which lives on through watching others live the one all children deserve. The children you sometimes dream about, and those who have already been born. The killing of a child is a moral injury and offense to all childhoods past and present, but especially to the children now leading movements to protect themselves and their peers, asking adults to simply move out of their future's way.

What Is the Present For?

JESSE NATHAN:

You have all of these interesting ways of thinking about what it means to talk about history, whether that's personal, national, geopolitical, or anything else. One metaphor you resist is the photograph—you make the point that you're not, in your writing, trying to make photographs of the past. What is it about a "photograph of the past" that you want to avoid? And what is the "present" for?

WENDY XU:

I'm terribly afraid of freezing my memories. I want them to stay liquid and permeable, even if that also means vulnerable to disturbance or corruption, intrusion, change, inaccuracy. I want them open to expansion, recontextualization.

As utilitarian objects I like photographs as much as anybody else, I like to look at them and express my little surprises at what someone was wearing, was it really that sunny that day, look at the cake on her face! As a metaphor for the past, or the Past, importantly, maybe I find a photograph too inert, too finished, unrevisable. I also don't write to revise the past, but to wade through all the pasts that my own past absorbs and is charged with keeping. My father's past, my mother's. The past someone else lived because on June 1, 1989, I came to live my actual past, in America. The spaces that act left open. The spaces it closed. That past speaks too. As a writer and daughter and immigrant I feel myself made of all these intersecting stories, so I'm averse to the singularness of the metaphor. All metaphors are clunky, admittedly. I think I conclude, in a poem at least, that the idea of a form (metaphor) that can "hold" the past itself is "an idea too elegant to exist," so maybe the real metaphor is air. Dissipating mist. A sandcastle of the past, I could have written, but that's . . . bad writing!

There's a self-implicating irony to the metaphor of a photograph that I like as well—I know much of the history of the country where I was born through photographs. How could I not. I didn't learn about Tiananmen Square through hushed conversations with my parents; I saw a photo of Tank Man in an American civics textbook in Iowa. I was like, What is that? I think I've stood in that square before. I definitely have. I recognize the streetlamps. But there was nothing there. There was certainly no trace of violence. Air. Mist.

In my poetry I hope I'm after something less tenable than a photograph, a depiction that risks rupture, denies comfort, holds simultaneous pasts.

My process is to grow a poem entirely from a singular catalyzing image that I either see, or that I see in a memory. I differentiate between those to indicate that sometimes the poem springs from the present, and sometimes from the past. Their genesis and their subject matter are two entirely different things. Many of my memories are pocked full of holes, as are my parents' memories, and I tend to write into those holes or around their outlines until the poem is filled up with its own goneness. Somewhere I wrote, "We don't remember how we got here, so have woven a beautiful story of replacement." It's true. I don't remember a thing. But some of the pasts pulsing in that We, do. Together we write that line, and others.

I wonder what the Present is for too. And who it's for. You could convince me that as an idea it's mostly for selling you weird products on Instagram, no? Live for the Moment. No Time Like the Present. Live in the Now. Age-Defying Wrinkle Cream. Live Laugh Love. Seize the Day. Seize the Land. Seize It All. Manifest Destiny. Maybe the Present is for Americans, tidy belief systems about individualism, exceptionalism, neoliberal bootstrappers. The past is fraught too, don't get me wrong, it can touch nostalgia dangerously. But I love its inevitability. That everything is always becoming the past, instant by instant, forever. As a poet who feels in exile from the Present (as a promise, as a violent optimism), I allow my poems to be past-facing, and oriented toward a narrative multiplicity that I hope discomfits Americana.[1]

Mignon, or, Further Notes on the Past

For fear of being discovered as one who writes poor, who writes bad, who writes lines so sentimental and excessively familiar that she would be laughed out of the institutions and lands where she resides. Probably for the best. *Death to the institutions that made me, long live the me that was made.*

When I was a child I couldn't descend from the top of the metal slide to the bottom (didn't even need to walk could have just slid down on my butt) without keeping my mother in my line of sight. I entered the covered slide and immediately began to cry, sliding and my skin burning a little on the back of my legs until I emerged from beneath the orange plastic down below, ran to grab my mother's leg. She'd congratulate me and pinch my mosquito bites and when we arrived back at home rub cut garlic halves on them making me feel like a soft little loved filet, little *mignon*, my mother's little meat dish whose personality would not come out without some coaxing, and maybe didn't have one to begin with, that was not simply fear of living without my mother.

Little soft meat that sits beside me at the desk, kicking legs in the air, one foot resting sometimes on the cat and it bothers her, little mignon with no personality until she found some pages to listen to her crying and the turnings of the little planet in her mind.

But other things too are the past. Are between you and it. Mothers become mothers when nobody wants them to be anything else, I thought to myself, and if it's not true I'd never know, sitting against the window and nodding off into a dream I won't remember.

What did I mean by the past? I meant the essential non-future that I live inside, the suspended forever that could never be the present, the alchemy of time constantly trying to leave me, when I catch up to anything I am already in my own past. *It* and its own evaporation, of course. I also meant specific disgraces and personal sorrows, isn't that what you meant too? When I look at you I see that we were born on different continents, the soil that someone walked on to carry you home from the hospital was chemically different, we're chemically different because of air, the pathogens that circulate in us like language, some toxic and some something else, definitely something else is keeping you alive than me but I can't quite see what it is.

Writing is the most embarrassing of all embarrassments, making work out of all others. The past embarrasses the future.

In my pathogen we say *qí hu nán xìa*, or *you're riding that tiger now and it would be dangerous to dismount*, how could you, as in how could you stop now, and how *could* you, the wrongness of your having begun in the first place. You stubborn thing who writes, why write about any of it, what's the point, why when Uncle died would you begin again inside those memories of the onion soup with pork bones, Uncle's shoulders jutting in incompatible directions, the permanent yellow stain under his eyes. Why start. Why write. And all that came out was another poem, the beast must be ridden. How could you.

Where do you go to get a personality? Mignon is always thinking, shirks some responsibilities to hide under the covers with the cat she'd like to have someday, with books, with a gloomy sense of indecency about how she should expect to be treated by others someday. I'm a little chubby meat and I like to read. Start there. I don't go sledding in the winter because there's something particularly threatening about English coming down the hill at top speed.

And what would it say about me if I were happy after all, happiness at a time like this? I think. I think about the past even now, there goes that sentence and this one slipping off the deck and into the dark water, it's oily is what it is, the past is always shiny with something sinister like the runoffs of a corporation or a cruise-boat full of pathogenic people dancing crazily, and all this goes into the water as well. Sentences are cannibals if you do them right, there was a painting of a Zen serpent eating itself in the bathroom of the café where I used to go and pretend to work when I was at my loneliest, and had received my college degree and was thinking oh no, now what, am I so embarrassing that I will become a writer?

Mignon was so often alone with herself and practicing improvisations of the future. Could she be as logical as men, *pathological*, supposing that to be practical begets something desirable: men at the harbor looking out over the water at the boats bobbing in green, frothing around the edges. Feeling free. Freer than most. Men belonging to themselves with divinity ahead, godliness, something really real.

The ears of the rabbit twitch like a satellite in my dream, I wrote that, it rotates to pick up a signal from behind itself which is the past catching up to me, is it not? Rabbit who lives with that beautiful woman up there on the craggy pocked face of the moon, she of the monstrous wanting, gray and blotched, I used to look up at her from my father's shoulders with eye pressed to the magnification tube and the ceiling retracted over us, the moon a land I would never go, not like this one where we all got stuck, stayed too long. They get you with the paperwork, you fill it out and they stick it in your eye, you're here to stay, congratulations.

But I was telling you about how mignon is more strange than cute, more filet-off-the-ol'-block than adorable, little cut of meat from her mother's womb raised on leafy greens and rice. Who is always sorry. Who is always of the stance of sorry. Who follows me to the public pool and floats there with one foot hanging off the security inflatable rope in a warm spot of pee, someone else's pee that mignon is still sorry for, sorry she couldn't keep its unpleasantness to herself.

How many are you, mignon? Who holds you to you, and do you write through air or do your speaking parts write through you? Do you have an easy time of it, ever? What did you inherit through the misjudging of time and place? Is there a charge in the air around violence that is elemental, ornate, supposed? Can you speak? Can you remember you correctly? Is it roomy there, florid, viscous, in the past? Do you clunk with potential and does it hurt you? Your caterpillar feet pushed into sneakers.

The embarrassment of writing is related to the embarrassment of mother, which helps me to understand my mother's embarrassment in an entirely new dimension. My mother must have wanted to mother, or can I accept that there are ambivalent mothers? Mothers who don't have any explanation for how they feel, who project their big sonorous moods from here in perpetuity, to the pigeons playing double in shit outside the window. A little hilltop that recollects bigger hilltops. I know this and yet I believe my mother wanted badly to be my mother, and thus poured most of her life's energy into me and it's this innate embarrassment, this desire she couldn't escape to mother, that courses through me, and which I feel acutely, when I am writing, when I am trying very hard to mother myself. The embarrassments never end, the preparation for it, the planning, the writing, and abandoning of all previous plans for a delusional state of spontaneity, the apology to and reconciliation with the contagion of writing, the shame when it disobeys, the joy when it cries and wants to be held.

Thus could I tolerate something a little bit disgusting, confused, oily and unpopular, a thing like mignon, the way my mother tolerated me? Thus I fear I'm fit to be a writer, not a mother. I had looked at all those discontinued lines, lamplight softly fading and some music still vibrating in the strings. How long has it been since last winter which never did come to light? It was the day the past came to an end, beneath us the earth was verbing around in color, and I felt a sympathetic twitch in my monolid.

Only when it seems to me it won't eat me, the air, its aliveness, shoving the flowerpot from the ledge, then I can write in my book, as that summer when a line of breath from between the lips escaped and became an angry march. Writing natural as forgetting. Troubling, disobedient work.

I cherished all the lines mignon ever wrote for me, the cut of her forehead in profile embellishes itself in sun, is really miraculous. From now on I'll take her to the doctor for a scrape or a fall, to the park at leaf-dropping time, the pink words fluttery and blowing off the branches—whoosh—whoosh—whoosh—yellow and the sound of it blurring. She could spin on her big toe smiling if she wants, mignon ever tapping out these messages on my palm. So I had my hand on the cracked rivulets phone screen, and raised it, and spoke Hi, mama. Love you.

Notes for a Canceled Short Lecture on Reversible and Coded Form(s)

Bei Dao, Su Hui, and Emily Lee Luan

There's an intersection I've been considering lately, between forms that are either participatory, "reversible" (more on that later), or multidirectional, and poems that are *coded*, either *for* a single reader (for your eyes only!), or, against interpretation *by* nefarious forces. Perhaps in the case of the poem coded for only a single reader to understand, the entirety of the poet and reader's shared history, along with the understanding that both parties will correctly emphasize the same experiences from among innumerable choices, function as the priceless key. The security of such a poem has been written in each moment since poet and reader first crossed paths.

The romance of such a key and the thoughts it might trigger in us about love and individuality aside, a coded poem may also importantly contain its own plausible deniability, especially when deniability is all that stands between the poet's criticism and state-issued punishment. The poet in this case need not *not* say, but cannot *say* without first building doubt about the saying into the poem itself. The poem must deny itself, or at least feign inability to understand itself, while it says itself. This kind of veiled, covert, and intentionally obfuscated speech asks us to raise our understanding of the stakes of poems that can be read "in different ways." Some ways have surely always led to violence or punishment.

To suggest that speaking vaguely, or in the language of generality, is merely a politically neutral craft choice is akin to suggesting that the passive voice has never been used to obscure violence and deflect blame. The passive voice is in fact exceedingly good at both obscuring and deflecting, concerned with plausible deniability at all times as it insists that things *happened*, things *were done*. If the sentence doesn't *do*, who can be accused? But what some poems "get away with" when speaking vaguely or in generalities is safety. It may critique the state or antagonize power while denying any subtextual meaning to its images, despite working in an art form that foregrounds the subtextual potential of all language.

The Chinese dissident-poet-in-exile Bei Dao (born 1949 in Beijing) is one such writer of poems that teem with allusion and vivid symbolism, always privileging mood and sensation over exposition. Barred from returning to China after the events of June 4, 1989, which the Chinese state accused him of helping to incite, Bei Dao has continued to write movingly of lineage, exile, memory, and his own youth growing up in China. In his work, the past is both lethargic and aggressive, and memory doesn't soothe as much as it "barks."[1] Most moving and skillful to me is an early poem "Notes from the City of the Sun,"[2] a series of short image fragments that follow large single-word thematic headers like "Youth," "Love," "Art," and "Fate." While some words such as "Labor" precede straightforwardly representative images ("A pair of hands, encircling the earth"),[3] others are more subtly ambiguous and provocative. Take for example "Youth," which is followed by "Red waves / drown a solitary oar,"[4] conjuring a defiantly anti-Chinese (anti-CCP at least) image of one-against-many. One is heroic and defiant (a motif that the CCP is sensitive to) while the malevolent red waves continue to threaten. Is this how the poet sees "youth" in his native China? In the absence of a lyric I, or expository language, the question and critique hang tantalizingly. Another stanza, "Freedom," is depicted as "Torn scraps of paper / fluttering,"[5] evoking the aftermath of something darker than celebration, nearing an image of detritus or debris, arguably carnage, the price of freedom itself?

Most evocative is the poem's final stanza, where "Living" is simply "A net."[6] A tool for capture, or that which saves the life of a falling man by catching him? The infinite braided strands that together make up humanity? If you want to know, the poem seems to reply: Who's asking?

A quick and interesting pedagogical interlude about translation, lest I forget—in 1983 Bonnie S. McDougall translated the poem's penultimate stanza as follows:

Motherland

Cast on a shield of bronze
she leans against a darkening museum wall[7]

The most recent translation was revised to the word "blackened" in the final line to describe the museum wall, substantially altering (or improving, depending on who you ask) the visual connotations of the image as a whole. A wall may be darkening due to falling shadows, the onset of evening, and an English reader likely will not read suspicious cause into the image. It may not even seem a particularly mysterious or evocative visual scene. But in context with the previous stanza, "blackened" becomes highly suggestive and seems to connote the aftermath of a violent conflict, a fire, or a revolutionary struggle. The previous stanza reads:

Peace

In the land where the king is dead
the old rifle sprouts branches and new shoots
and becomes a cripple's cane[8]

The poet's image of "peace" here features the slightly magical if familiar transformation of a discarded weapon into a tree branch, repurposed as a walking aid. But we might intuit that if such peace, impossible under monarchy, was hard won with armed conflict, that the cane-user themself might be a wounded soldier, and that the "blackened" museum wall in the following stanza is still a high price to pay for one's "Motherland." To defend her? Or to rescue her?

As a fluent Mandarin speaker who is illiterate in reading and writing the language, I too am at the mercy of Bei Dao's attentive translators. In the early translation of "Youth," red waves initially only "soak" a solitary oar, before undergoing a suggestive revision to "drown"[9] that escalates the political implications of the imagery. In the later rendering, there is no question as to the fate of the One who dares to face many.

There's no conversation about the romance of a "for your eyes only" coded poem that doesn't include the fourth-century Chinese poet Su Hui's famous "Star Gauge" poem, an impossibly intricate twenty-nine-character by twenty-nine-character gridded poem embroidered in silk.

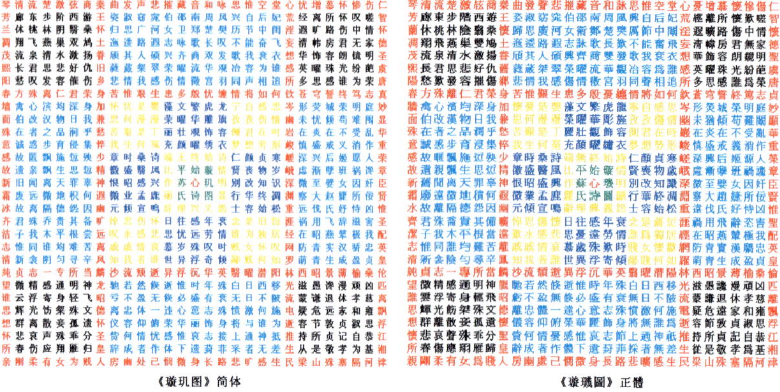

Fig. 4. Layout of Su Hui's "Star Gauge" poem

The image left uses simplified Chinese characters; the image right uses traditional characters.[10]

Each colored quadrant or boundary represents a particular internal rhyme scheme unto itself, but the poem can also be read in any direction within sections, culminating in an estimated 12,000 possible unique poems. The "Star Gauge," named after fourth-century celestial charts, was neither then nor now simply a "make your own poem" experience, and is governed by the reader's choices within parameters of directional flow and color.

Su Hui is legendary in China for how she employed the "Star Gauge"—after her husband took a concubine against her wishes and moved far away for work, she wrote the poem and sent it to him as a letter. The legend tells that the poem achieved its goal; Su Hui's husband returned to her, and without the concubine.[11] We can choose to imagine that the power of the poem is in fact its 11,999 obfuscations, designed for any reader who may intercept the poem, with one "true" reading legible only to her husband, convincing (or threatening?) enough to bring him back home. Any reader who is not Su Hui's husband is fundamentally *wrong*, themselves a bad key, and although they are welcome to enjoy the 12,000 possibilities of the Star Gauge, they are only enjoying the surplus and misdirection built into the poem's fierce private world. Our participation is a consolation and our misunderstanding co-creates the poem's deep intimacy. The poem ironically offers true *choice* via multidirectional readings to all readers save one, the philandering husband whose own knowledge of the shared life he abandoned unlocks Su Hui's message.

In 2023 I spoke at length with poet Emily Lee Luan, whose first book 回 / *Return*[12] is explicitly inspired by Su Hui and valences of reversibility, among many other things. Asked about longing, melancholia, and the cinematic quality of her work, we had the following exchange:

ELL

I think my poems try to understand internal emotional change through the external world—that might be why image and scene are so central. If you look at something for long enough, then you might be able to understand what's happening within you.

Another impulse I have to this question is related to nostalgia. It's the only word we have for looking back and longing, but it's a romantic, sentimental longing. 回 / *Return* is centered on memory and looking back, but it's actually anti-nostalgia in many ways. Well, I'm politically against nostalgia, first of all.

WX

Me too.

ELL

Right, nostalgia's only reserved for some. So I'm trying to carve out a definition of longing for the past that is a complex looking-back, and the filmic quality is likely informed by that.

WX

"Against nostalgia" is so essential, for the reasons you bring up. You have this great way of depicting "return" as an act in your book that's not always easy, tidy, or utopian. When the river returns in your world, for example, it returns "brutally" as often as it might beautifully.

I think your work challenges something that so often gets projected onto literature depicting displacement, colonization, immigration, et cetera, which is the idea that "return" must be the central nostalgic (almost childlike) fixation and goal. And your return is so much more uneasy than that. Are there other valences of return that are interesting to you as a poet, besides the brutal and the beautiful?

ELL

My paternal grandfather migrated to Taiwan post–Chinese Civil War, from northern China. And I always heard stories growing up about how he was separated from his family and siblings for decades, who he left behind. When I wrote the poems in 回 / *Return*, I was really grappling with this reality that, while I longed to return to a Taiwan that wasn't mine—that was my parents'—my grandfather had wanted to return to his homeland, which was not Taiwan. So immediately this idea of "return" is complicated, that my grandfather was looking back in a different direction than I was.[13]

For those who migrate, immigrate, flee, or are otherwise politically displaced, "multidirectionality" is literal. The cardinal directions of this earth correspond to homes, people, and objects left behind, and the "different directions" we find ourselves pointed toward are often against our will. To reverse, give permission to reverse, or alternatively exert extreme control *over* reversal and the direction of a poem's movement is, as Luan implies, to attempt to transcend nostalgia and romanticized longing. If this attempt is cinematic as an *affect*, we might understand that as a product of its failed (i.e., impossible) realism, rather than a decorous aesthetic.

I often wish that during our already long and delightfully meandering interview, I'd had time to include one more question for Emily—to ask, for her, how *to return* differentiates itself in some essential way from *to go back*, if it does at all. I often punt the question around in my head, putting aside obvious differences in diction or formality between the two. Those are concerns of language, and I wonder if what I want to ask is ultimately a metaphysical question. What is the philosophical nature of a past one can or cannot *return* to, and does this necessitate singular or multiple past(s)? Why does *to go back* connote a reality of failure or defeat, only partially explained by the racist trope of being told *to go back* to X country of origin? I'm not convinced that in language, in this language, we're allowed *to go back* triumphantly, to go back with dignity. We may only *return* with it.

In Chinese, both the geographic and emotional direction of *return* as a command must be specified in relation to the one who commands it. 回 is simply *return* as an act, *húi* in the Chinese Pinyin phonetic system, but it would be grammatically odd to tell somebody to *húi*. A native speaker would say either "húi lài," which means definitively to return to *me*, or *me here*. It combines *return* with the command *come*. *Húi qù* means return *there*, or more accurately *return* and *go*, as in go away *from me*, and away from here. Return is thus always relational in Chinese, a verb that does not guarantee reunion as it may either imperil or restore connection between parties. If one returns home, for example, and wants to declare her presence to a loved one in the house she will say, I "húi lài le" (*le* is an add-on that indicates a state of being), meaning I've returned home to you here, to your presence. But if the traveler finds herself mistaken, and the rooms of the house are actually empty, she might pick up the phone and call her loved one, reporting instead that I "húi dào le," meaning I've returned to where you are not.

None of this suggests that English doesn't contain its own elegant solutions, the greatest of which is the ease of the phrase, shouted upon entering the house and dropping one's bag, with hope but without guarantee that anybody will hear: "I'm home!"

One of Luan's most spectacular "reversible" poems is titled "She's the Only One Who Hears Me Sing,"[14] with the words in the title stylized into a closed circle such that "Sing" brings a reader right back to "She's" and invites her to read through. The poem is an evocative riff on a reversible Chinese poem form called 反覆 ("to turn and return") illustrated in the figure in Luan's own handwriting for an essay on reversing for *futurefeed*:[15]

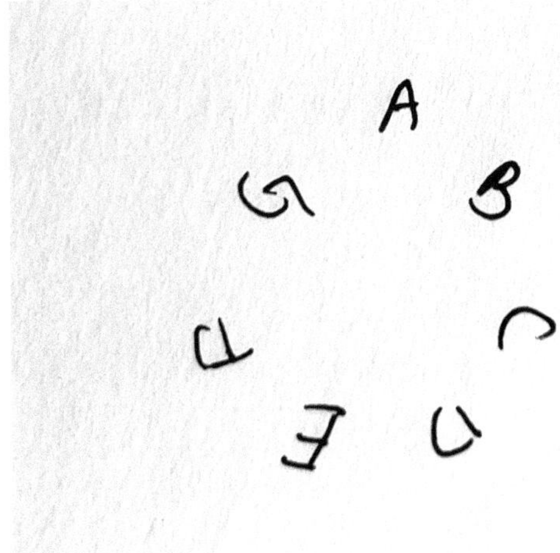

Fig. 5. "Turn and return" poem form in Luan's handwriting

In the "turn and return" form, each letter represents one Chinese character, and to enact the poem, a reader begins with A and reads clockwise, then reverses and reads from A counterclockwise. Then the same repeats starting with B, then C, and so on, with the effect feeling a bit like using a rotary telephone. Playing with and loosening this form, Luan's poem begins:

She's the only one who hears me sing.
The only one who hears me singing, she.

Only one, who hears my song?
One hears me sing—no, she's the only.

Who, me? I'm my only.
Hear me sing her only song.

I sing, and there's my only, hearing.
Sing her to only.[16]

Luan's reversible poem begins in a pattern of A B C D E F G, followed by B C D E F G A, with allowances throughout for excluding words, changing word tense, and adjusting punctuation. A reader would be correct in thinking that though it's interesting to know the inner mechanisms of this poetic form, that knowledge is far from required to appreciate the dizzy torque of the poem's energy. Though the poem faithfully follows the restriction of seven core words throughout (She's the Only One Who Hears Me Sing), Luan attests that writing reversible poems required that she free herself from "mechanics of conjunctions, conjugation, articles, the meaning-making of linear form" in order to escape from what she calls "just walking backwards." "To *really* reverse"[17] required a loosening of English's grammatical rules governing word sequence and fixed parts of speech. If Su Hui's reversible poem contained the promise of one true or true(r) poem, meant only for her husband to understand, Luan's poem sets all possible realities into motion simultaneously with a spin of her title's wheel.

Part of reversibility's charm, then, is its naturally occurring ambiguity and subject confusion, as "She" can possess "Me," "Her," "She Who Sings,"

Fig. 6. Stylized title for "She's the Only One Who Hears Me Sing"

"My Only," "My Onely," or simply "One" spontaneously, and "I" is both singing, heard singing, and listening to the song of another. The reversible poem doesn't return to any fixed point, and doesn't concern itself with primary and secondary versions. Though the seven foundational words of "She's the Only One Who Hears Me Sing" are fixed in number, thus cannot *multiply*, the wheel of their relations goes on spinning.

My interest in the possibilities and limits of return was seeded outside poetry, and continues to grow. Since 2017, I've done a particular mode of talk therapy called IFS, or Internal Family Systems, with the help of an IFS-trained therapist. IFS has a simple premise, one that I've always felt was easy to accept intellectually and more challenging to engage emotionally—that each of us is made up of many parts, each of which is unique in their wishes, desires, fears, goals, and talents. We're not so much one singular and unified whole, as we might like to believe, but rather a complex internal family that love, support, contradict, fight, and even shame one another at different times, just like an "external" family. IFS as a modality would indeed be well advertised by Whitman's famous "I contain multitudes." Some parts are young and vulnerable, while others take on protective or managerial roles in order to prevent imagined disasters from happening to the whole family system. Often, parts disagree strongly. Ask anybody if they have ever, when faced with a tough decision, thought to themselves something like "a *part* of me wants to go on that trip, but another *part* of me wants to cancel and catch up on work." Most people would agree that yes, this is a common experience. We already intuitively understand that the self can be divided, and that *parts* of us can hold contradictory beliefs, even extreme or distorted beliefs that feel too true to overcome.

Something important about our parts, my therapist reminds me, is that none are bad. All have benevolent intentions and are trying their best. Childlike internal parts, just like external children in the world, don't understand what they don't understand, and can't be shamed or shouted into submission. What all children need, external or internal, is care, and this care is the work of a lifetime. In my experience, inside and outside of IFS, *care* more often than not involves *return*.

In IFS we return, in our minds, to former experiences of extreme emotion, distress, dysregulation, and the feelings and beliefs about ourselves that were produced. For me, this has sometimes involved the difficult childhood experiences one would expect, and other times I have "returned" to a memory that for most of my adult life I have considered normal, unremarkable even. In this exercise "to return" does not mean to relive, or to relitigate, emotionally or literally. I may see myself there, in the memory which was a site of fear or heightened emotion, and may even feel flooded with difficult sensations, but am protected by the knowledge that time cannot reverse. I cannot *really* reverse, go back, nor be sent back. Because I can never be a child again, thus I may return to myself as a child as an adult, with the tenderness and patience that I needed as a child. "You are the one that you've been waiting for" is a refrain from IFS that de-pathologizes both being separated from yourself and needing to return to yourself, a cyclical movement that is both optimistic and melancholy.[18]

Part of my experience of immigration, having been brought to the United States as a small child, is fearing the rise of the desire to undo my parents' decision. Were I to reverse course, as they say, what has it all been for? If this were an IFS session, and I were instead returning in my mind's eye, I would be greeted by myself at three years old, appearing in the mist of my impressionistic memories of Shandong, China. I would reassure her that I'm not here to relive her leaving, or relitigate the decision to take her away. I would be free to stay with her as long as I wanted, to look around, to feel long-forgotten feelings suddenly burst open for me.

I could ask myself at three years old what she needs, what she thinks, what she fears, and be surprised to find that I can conjure different conditions for her. That I can change the warmth of the sun on the sidewalk to be stronger or weaker, that I can make it rain or hail, that I can draw faces in the sky, that I can cook dishes I have never learned to make. I'll have time to try again, to get it just right, and to find that indeed I am the one I've been waiting for.

I think I am describing poetry, and one of the many ways it is made. Its purpose is not to relive or relitigate, but to discover, through visitation, *how it was*, how one suffered or didn't or caused the suffering of others, how one lived a single moment or a single year, and to bring that news back to ourselves in the present. We change how *it* was each time we return, and thus how *I* was, and who I am in the present. All the more reason to return again.

Wendy Xu and Emily Lee Luan on Return, Form, and Longing

I met Emily Lee Luan in the winter of 2020, in Brooklyn, through the Asian American Writers' Workshop, where she was a 2020 Margins Fellow. During Emily's fellowship year, when we met regularly, our conversations at length about family, poetry, the stories we keep and carry, and the essential mystery of what writing makes possible buoyed and inspired me. The spark of friendship is unpredictable, and thus is a gift to both person and poetry when it appears.

At the time Emily was already at work on the project that would become 回 / *Return* (Nightboat, 2023), her debut collection of poetry just published in April. A book of both startling intimacy and formal excitement, neither compromising the other, 回 / *Return* is an assured and moving debut that navigates the murk (and heft) of the past, dissatisfied with easy nostalgia. Her work ranges freely across fragment, lyric, memoir, dreamscape, collage, documentary language, visual poetry, and the thrillingly uncategorizable, in poems that owe as much to Theresa Hak Kyun Cha's *Dictee* as they do to Petrarch's sonnets. Throughout, 回 / *Return* takes up the Chinese "reversible poem" as central conceit, using it to explore the limits of narrative desire, racial melancholia, and nostalgia itself.

Each time I speak with Emily I'm moved anew by her political clarity and her poetry's elegant conceptual scaffolding. I consider this conversation, which took place on May 24, 2023, in Brooklyn, to be but a snippet of a more endless one.

WENDY XU:

Congratulations on 回 / *Return*. I can't believe it's here! How's all this been for you so far?

EMILY LEE LUAN:

So wonderful, and terrifying. I somehow thought I would be immune to the emotional experience of putting out a book, but of course I've felt the full range.

WX:

Yes to the full range. We've spoken before, elsewhere, about the difficulty of "What is your writing process like?"-type questions, and tempted as I am to ask you that now, maybe that exact difficulty is more interesting. People like to know writers' processes, I get that. But for the poet it can feel nearly impossible to speak on it. How have you been managing and answering that question, or evading it, now that 回 / *Return* is just published?

ELL:

This question is hard because when I think back to times I've actually been writing, each time looks very different. And right now, I have to contend with the fact that I *haven't* been writing. So I try and answer these kinds of questions in a way that shows the volatility of my writing process.

WX:

Totally. Are you in a period of *not* writing now with the book coming out?

ELL:

Yeah, I haven't written in a really long time.

WX:

That's great. I'm actually happy for you.

ELL:

I really appreciate that. I've only recently gotten past the self-punishment phase of not writing.

WX:

I could just be projecting, but when you were anticipating 回 / *Return* coming out, did you ever have that thought that finally you would *get* to have this period of rest and not writing? You know what I mean? Obviously you have to not write to write. And productivity culture is like "this is the one time you're *allowed* to not write, only after you've—"

ELL:

Actually done the thing.

WX:

Exactly. And it comes out and it's like, oh my god. Everybody's focused on *it* and finally, *you* get some rest or something. Or are you not experiencing that?

ELL:

Well, after the book got taken, I immediately went on a series of writing residencies. I was able to focus in on new projects, which has been really helpful—to look forward to new poems so you're not dwelling too much. But now that the book is out I'm realizing just how much work I've put in; I keep describing it as a second job. That realization has definitely let me forgive myself for not writing or even reading that much.

WX:

Well, and you're taking care of the thing in a different way, right? It needs something different from you now. It just needs you to take it to the bookstore or take it to meet people, et cetera.

The beautiful cover of 回 / *Return* is on the table between us. I know that this is your mother's calligraphy, which is perfect. How did that happen? It just seems so important that a mark of her literal movements and brushstrokes grace the cover.

ELL:

My mom has been doing calligraphy for the past almost ten years. She's very much an artist—always making and crafting, and so calligraphy has been just another iteration of her practice.

Initially, we had computer-generated text of the characters on the cover. It took me a while to realize how complex a task it would be to put together the title 回 with the English "Return," as well as with my name in both English and Chinese. I want to shout out the incredible designers at Nightboat—Rissa Hochberger and Claire Zhang—for seeing the cover through, and for their patience!

We had to ask ourselves: "How do I get a reader to look at the character first before they look at the English?" It's important to me that a reader starts with the Chinese character—I was resistant to even putting the word "Return" on the cover. And the computer-generated version of the character wasn't offering the effect that it needed to. What you're saying about movement—that's exactly what was missing. Once we incorporated the calligraphy, it made so much more sense. I feel like I didn't need to describe to the designers the power of the Chinese characters, because they could *see* it in my mother's work.

WENDY XU:

In the poems you talk about that too, the brushstrokes and graphic quality of the characters, a series of movements that must be done in a certain order. I think that's the richness of the cover choice that I'm responding to—the character is a somatic mark, whereas hitting the computer button can also make the character for you, but that's different, like you're saying. It's not an embodied act.

ELL:

Also, if you think about the origins of Chinese poetry, at that time, calligraphy, landscape painting, and the poem are all part of one continuous craft, and the idea was that you could gain access to a higher realm through the practice of all three. In that way, enacting the Chinese character through calligraphy is the same process as writing a poem. I'm so glad you brought up the question of embodiment—I'm realizing just how important the calligraphy on the cover is.

WX:

Some background for this conversation is how we met, and my relationship to 回 / *Return*. We met in 2020 through the Asian American Writers' Workshop, where you were a Margins Fellow and working on the project that would eventually become 回 / *Return*. It was pandemic winter, and we used to meet up in Herbert Von King Park and sit outside and try to stay warm while talking about poetry and the manuscript. So

I've been able to love this book for a long time. I remember we lucked out, because other writers paired together by the Fellowship didn't live anywhere near each other so they had to meet on Zoom. We realized we lived in the same neighborhood and it was such a treat. That experience was a bright spot in a hard year. The book was still called *I Watch the Boughs* at the time, right?

ELL:

Yeah, it was.

WX:

I remember that my impression of meeting you and your work was like "Oh my god, this person is really assured about her work and these poems and the complex conceptual and emotional work it's doing." Like, good for her! But I'm checking myself now, that was all assumption. It was a crazy moment in time, so much uncertainty, and you were trying to bring this thing together. Do you remember where you actually were with 回 / *Return*, emotionally, or otherwise? Do you remember what you were thinking or feeling about it?

ELL:

I think I was feeling confident about the concept of the book, and that I had kind of sussed out its political and linguistic arguments for myself. I'd been working with the reversible poem for over a year at that point, and I knew deeply that that was the conceit that would tie the entire book together. But I didn't trust the poems. I think that's why it was so helpful to talk to you—at such length and in the freezing cold!—because I needed somebody to name what they saw in the book and level it with what I was hoping the poems did. I remember feeling this exact doubt when I thought to name the book 回—I think I even frantically emailed you.

WX:

Yeah. I remember!

ELL:

I was like, "Am I just doing a floofy performative thing?" I didn't trust that the book could hold up the title. Though it's also silly to put so much weight on the character, since it's only the market and world that we're in that tells us that to name a book in a different language is controversial or strange in any way—

WX:

But it feels like a gigantic choice or something.

ELL:

Yes. And it's just hard to see yourself very clearly at that stage.

WX:

Yes. And not to over-read the context of putting a book together in a pandemic, but it was such a time of isolation, distrust. It was hard to see anything clearly.

What I love about your multilingual poems is that the non-English language is not like just a sprinkle of racialized titillation for monolingual readers. It's not just ornamental, an accessory. I remember being so truly moved by your work because when I thought about my younger self, I didn't remember having access to the belief that it *could* be more than that if I were to write "American" poetry. Maybe you can't know, but what makes it so natural for you, that your first book would treat language(s) this way?

ELL:

My first answer to this is actually very simple. If you partake in any deep study of a language, you come to understand the complex beauty of that language. I grew up speaking Chinese and then studied Chinese for four years in college. There's so much power to the language, especially visually. I was seeing that in offering a translation or phonetic transliteration of Chinese in a poem, I was stripping the language of that power.

The task was then figuring out how I could put the language on the page and not have it be a placeholder, to *show* a reader that they *can* understand, outside of wanting to know a word's meaning or how it's pronounced.

A second simple but really important reason is that in my MFA, there were many of us who were working with multilingual poetry—

WX:

Oh, I love that.

ELL:

At Rutgers-Newark, the conversation in the classroom wasn't just, "Why is the language there?" It started with, "Okay, the language is on the page and now where do we go? What do we gain from it? How do we make sense of it?" I was never questioned for putting Chinese in my poems. If I didn't have that environment, maybe I wouldn't have continued putting Chinese in my poems. I don't know.

WX:

How important that the potentially othered language, in this case Chinese, doesn't have to doubly fight for its right to exist in the work. It has a presumed essentialness or something, once you've put it down.

ELL:

I love that. That's a great way to put it.

WX:

In a recent interview you spoke on something related to this, which is how readers might make different choices when coming across a language that they can't immediately read. You called it the "silence of non-recognition" and added that it's not the same as being "shut out" of a poem, that readers don't *have* to feel that they're not the intended audience just because they see non-English languages.[1] I agree, firstly! I'd even argue it can be a form of Orientalizing and othering the poem, to hastily decide "this is not for me" and cut off engagement. It seems subtly reactionary. I think that's why I was so moved by how you talked about it in that interview, the poem deserving more. Not to ask you to be prescriptive or anything, but is there something better or richer for a reader to do instead of just treating a "foreign" language like a brick wall?

ELL:

Really all I want from a reader is to look a little bit closer, instead of glossing over or moving quickly past the Chinese on the page.

One of the poems in the book, for example, plays with the phrases "捨得" and "捨不得" throughout. Some readers have told me, "Oh, I'm noticing the added character from the first phrase to the second and, within the context of the poem, I'm understanding that that first action *might* be negated in the second by the addition of that character." I love that that reader was willing to say, "Maybe that's wrong, but that's what I'm seeing. I'm willing to imagine a possibility for it; I'm taking the intentions of the Chinese as information." And in that, they're meeting me at my intention.

Let's say you have two people who don't speak the same language. You have to make that same leap, or else you're just not speaking to them or choosing not to understand them.

WX:

Yes, you're asking them first to just *stay*. And from there, for some vulnerability.

I assume the MFA at Rutgers-Newark was a formative experience, but I also want to make room to ask about other realms of experience that aren't reading poetry, studying poetry, degrees in poetry, etc., that inform 回 / *Return?* Are there invisible influences on the book that feel big?

ELL:

I've been thinking a lot about how the image-world of the book came to be, from pieced-together memories of family histories, photographs of my parents in Taiwan, my visits to the island when I was young, etc. And after writing the book I also (finally) started watching early Taiwanese New Wave films and was struck by the richness of scene in that time—Taiwan in the eighties and nineties.

WX:

It had a very specific look in cinema.

ELL:

Yes. Such a specific aesthetic, and it feels really true. I was seeing just how deeply the imagery of that time had been imprinted on me.

WX:

I've always found your work to be really cinematic, since we're talking about it, especially the Grandfather series of poems, which in 回 / *Return* are threaded throughout the collection as a kind of core narrative. Is there some inherent connection for you between the melancholia that you're investigating and a cinematic approach? What does the cinematic poem do for you that an expository poem can't? I always feel like I'm at the movies in your work. I'm really seeing it.

ELL:

The cinematic quality of the poems, how is that able to tell meaning beyond exposition?

WX:

Yes, why is it more emotive for you?

ELL:

Oh, such an interesting question. I think my poems try to understand internal emotional change through the external world—that might be why image and scene are so central. If you look at something for long enough, then you might be able to understand what's happening within you.

WX:

Oh, that's an elegant phrasing.

ELL:

Another impulse I have to this question is related to nostalgia. It's the only word we have for looking back and longing, but it's a romantic, sentimental longing. 回 / *Return* is centered on memory and looking back, but it's actually anti-nostalgia in many ways. Well, I'm politically against nostalgia, first of all.

WX:

Me too.

ELL:

Right, nostalgia's only reserved for some. So I'm trying to carve out a definition of longing for the past that is a complex looking-back, and the filmic quality is likely informed by that.

WX:

"Against nostalgia" is so essential, for the reasons you bring up. You have this great way of depicting "return" as an act in your book that's not always easy, tidy, or utopian. When the river returns in your world, for example, it returns "brutally" as often as it might beautifully.

I think your work challenges something that so often gets projected onto literature depicting displacement, colonization, immigration, etc., which is the idea that "return" must be the central nostalgic (almost childlike) fixation and goal. And your return is so much more uneasy than that. Are there other valences of return that are interesting to you as a poet, besides the brutal and the beautiful?

ELL:

My paternal grandfather migrated to Taiwan post–Chinese Civil War, from northern China. And I always heard stories growing up about how he was separated from his family and siblings for decades, who he left behind. When I wrote the poems in 回 / *Return*, I was really grappling with this reality that, while I longed to return to a Taiwan that wasn't mine—that was my parent's—my grandfather had wanted to return to *his* homeland, which was not Taiwan. So immediately this idea of "return" is complicated, that my grandfather was looking back in a different direction than I was.

WX:

Wow, yeah. And these motifs of incompatible return, grandfather, and emptiness all seem to triangulate each other. When I see the character 回 I see two nested emptinesses, double voids. But for you it's also a place of possibility or meeting: "a hole so deep I might one day meet him in the middle," speaking again about the speaker's grandfather.

ELL:

The poem where the speaker talks to the grandfather—"何處別魂銷?"—is in the center of the book. The speaker and the grandfather are in the hole together, or in that in-between space, in this case, between life and death. Much of the affect theory and writing on racial melancholia that spawned this book argues for looking at negative emotions (what Sianne Ngai also calls "ugly feelings"), like ambivalence, melancholy, disgust, etc., as generative. I've always wanted the book to be generative, even if it's looking at darkness or loss or sadness.

WX:

I think that's why I love that one visual poem so much. The one that is literally a hole, but the text is "I was born here," the hole literally spawning other holes.

ELL:

Proliferation is a word that's coming to mind.

WX:

Yes. Generative and proliferative . . . a force.

ELL:

I'm also reminded of the third space of language—in the void, there is no language, or language collapses in on itself, and so it's rich with communicative possibility. The hole or well produces sound in its echo. That also feels generative to me.[2]

Part Three

"Unfinished Is Business"

On Fandom and Stardom, Genre, Playing Your Role, and #9 Celtics Guard Derrick White; Coming to America

Student of Love

The mantra for this most recent season's playoff run by the Boston Celtics, the run that ended in a long-awaited championship and the hanging of the eighteenth banner, was *Different Here*, a pivot from the previous year's more declarative and intentional *Unfinished Business*. That season had ended in heartbreak, prolonging the business that had to be finished by a successful championship bid. As a writer, and a fan, I found *Different Here* to be middling and demure, even humble, a sort of "we're having a nice time here" mantra, lacking any of the bold bravado that I love about the NBA as a whole. *Different Here* is pointing to that ambiguous thing we call a team's "culture," and though all team cultures claim to be different, all team cultures are expected to tow the line of advertising a unique team culture. *Different Here* felt like it meant to gesture unthreateningly toward run-of-the-mill values like teamwork, sacrifice, perseverance, and determination, or what Celtics coach Joe Mazulla calls "mental toughness" any chance he gets.

The previous *Unfinished Business* delighted and moved me. It was the overconfident, swaggering, threatening, and painting-a-bullseye-on-it mantra that fans wanted after the *previous* year's successful trip to the finals ended in a loss. As stylized on the official team warm-up shirts, worn during every game, the "is" in the word "Unfinished" was meant to resemble the number "18" in a contrasting color, for the pursuit of Banner 18. But because of inscrutable graphic design choices, "is" continued to most resemble "is," only bolded, and it was impossible not to confidently read the shirt as Unfinished *Is* Business, emphasis in this case not mine, but the graphic's own. It's a stretch, but you could make an argument that the difficult-to-see "18" was an Easter egg of sorts, intentionally subtle so that only real fans, those that know exactly how many banners have been won by their Celtics, can spot it. But that suggests a reality where the designers were comfortable with a T-shirt that for majority of viewers would either read Unfinished Is Business, or Is Unfinished Business.

I loved the possibility of Unfinished Is Business almost as much as the correct mantra, its strangeness and evocative poeticism, a perfect equational statement of fact. "Unfinished" grows in size every time you say it, it threatens to even grow its own article, to be so self-important that it becomes The Unfinished, the proverbial, a cosmic That Which Cannot End. And if it's business, like standing on business, or when you *make it* your business, then the great Unfinished seems to grow yet again. Whatever you are still chasing, what you still have spirit and breath and belief to chase, is your business in this life. As the season went on, I couldn't find a single occasion to argue with it. Of course the practice of annual mantras for teams in the NBA is not really a matter of poetry, but one of marketing and merchandising, of attention and financial capture, but the league takes its job as writers seriously and churns out team narratives as well as compelling individual hero journeys every season. It's like your favorite television show that's been airing forever.

I do a kind of therapy called Internal Family Systems (IFS) that starts from the premise that each of us contains many parts, each holding unique desires, stresses, beliefs, fears, and hopes. They are often born from intense or monumental experiences in our lives, good or bad, and they interact with each other exactly how an external family does. They compete without meaning to, they disagree, they form alliances and groups, they make up, they bully each other, they struggle and succeed in various combinations that are fluidly changing. Every part has strengths, weaknesses, just like us. They *are* us, of course, and most people wouldn't find it too strange to accept the statement that sometimes a part of you wants to do one thing, but another part equally wants to do the opposite. Internal conflict is natural, and universal. So is teamwork. Basketball and the desire to *be* less cohesive, to stop fetishizing myself as needing to be inherently *one*, came into my life at the same time.

People teach you how to love what you're new to loving, and if you're lucky they will delight in your tutelage. They are compasses for your attention and sometimes possess an orthodoxy you will either choose to embrace or reject. Some are surely anti-models, the kind of fan (fair-weather, sociopathic, whatever it is) you hope never to be. I've always found myself accepting their various wisdoms piously in the moment and waiting to evaluate their merits. There's a thrill too in rebelling against some settled fandom truth, like a teenager on a streak of petulance. But you are most importantly always learning, and as your love grows it is a testament to theirs.

My brother-in-law loves the Chicago Bulls, which in the year 2024 means he's been suffering for a very long time. But it's his hatred for the Celtics that teaches me the most, as it can emerge in the form of comedy, parody, passionate dissent, or my favorite, straightforward analysis, during which I am his devoted student attendant to his knowledge and seniority, his devotion to the art form. When he takes the time to teach me how to play NBA 2K, and realizes that I don't know the five-second inbounding rule, he is teaching me how to love better and more attentively. He and my sister took me to my first Celtics game, in Boston, at TD Garden, the mothership for the best (most misbehaved, deranged) basketball fans in the world. He wore a Chicago Bulls shirt, naturally, and befriended a seatmate of similar disposition in our section. At the time I was the kind of infant fan who decidedly does *not* want to see good basketball, I wanted to see a beatdown and showmanship and that night I was granted my heart's wish. It was thrilling, truthfully, to try on being the kind of fan who isn't normal about basketball, can't be normal about her love, a zealot absolutely unreachable by critique, discussion, sportsmanship, perhaps even real happiness or satisfaction, whose love makes her unyielding and irrational, as love of all kinds often does.

But I'm not quite that kind of fan anymore, and in the present moment, it's the end of the 2024 NBA playoffs and the team I love is one game away from winning it all, from the mountaintop. I feel an unexpected reluctance and sadness to see this victory, which feels inevitable with the team that's been assembled, which only leads me to think about all the players who were sent off into the wilderness in order to bring about this win. Marcus Smart, the most devastating loss, the walking embodiment of "unfinished business" mentality, and Robert Williams III, the

Time Lord made of glass, his bumbling shaggy kid joy, the grin after the slams, the bouncing step, the absolute refusal to keep his hair out of his face when he plays. Even Sixth Man of the Year Malcom Brogdon, who I learned to love for his austerity, his sense of purpose and seriousness, his occasional leaks of vulnerability and desire to belong more, to be seen as a winner, who felt perhaps accurately that he had gone to war for his team only to be sent adrift with Rob in the offseason.

Pains of Genre

When the ball is moving, as if tossed between the limbs of a single sentient creature, I and all other fans are happy. When the balls seems heavy or worse slippery, when it deadens and slogs through the air, arcs too high and slow, or flat, when the sounds are just wrong, the bricks are throwing themselves, fans suffer and try to hold out for the next run. Writing about it kills something and of course it does, because ball movement is the opposite of exposition. It is a happening, not a telling, a spontaneity. In a poem, I have tried to write about the Celtics and their dynamism, only managing the slogan-rific line "Go C's," both the most vacuous and meaningful language I could think of, but to a fan is hardly a limpid phrase, it's simply everything felt and wished. It's an ideal totality, our whole universe.

I've been trying and failing to write a fan letter to #9 Celtics guard Derrick White, my favorite player, for several years. Epistolary writing and fandom have seemed a tricky match, and if I'm being honest, one I'm not sure how to approach. Fan mail is ostensibly about proximity, overcoming the distance between yourself and your idol, initiating the possibility that somewhere your idol may learn that you exist on earth. It's The Creation of Adam, except nobody is really reaching back to Adam. If God has a responsive staff person, the fan may find themselves the lucky recipient of a long but impersonal stock reply letter and a photocopied autograph. Naturally I have wondered if epistolary *poetry* might be the solution; dare I send my favorite player a poem in his honor? But this question contains its own answer, as I couldn't imagine writing a poem with intention to *honor* at all, something that I associate despots and dictators with wanting. Knowing already what I want to say, the possibility of saying it in a poem is also cut off—curiosity about what will happen is undeniably the force that brings me to the page. The more I know, the more impossible the poem grows.

I first saw Derrick White (D White) on *Sportscenter* just after he was traded to Boston from the San Antonio Spurs, giving a virtual postgame interview. He was nervous and having what seemed clearly to be an experience of fear, speaking with difficulty and some discomfort, his now famously enormous "emoji eyes" wide and unblinking. He was not a star, and he was playing streakily with his new team, alternating nights playing bright and dull, struggling to find his footing midseason with a group of players who had been together for a long time, some almost since their rookie year. I had wondered at the time if perhaps it was altruism that led *Sportscenter* to give a minimally impactful role player the interview, or maybe nobody else was willing. He started every sentence with "errrm" and seemed bewildered and plain, a human incarnation of the word *minor*.

Everyone loves an underdog but only at the moment of the upset, the coup of social strata, the overcoming of their unremarkable nature in dazzling fashion. If we really just loved an underdog for being an underdog, we would all be glued to G League games, the NBA's development league where some rookies also play in order to develop their skills. For reasons of both intuition and projection, I'm sure, I felt that I was watching an underdog lacking confidence but not skill, someone of great potential who only needed more time in the right environment. As a fan, like all fans, I understood myself to be of great importance to this effort.

At moments I felt I could write to D White without flattening him into the Beloved Subject of the epistolary and lyric tradition(s), that I could resist using him as a lyrical interlocutor between myself and myself. That is, I believed I could write to him *to* him, instead of writing to him *to* me, and without turning him into a mirror in which to cultivate my own self-knowledge. My interest in the genre of the fan letter thus began, a form I had never yet experienced any desire to explore. As a younger person I didn't have idols in sports or music, not even inherited from my parents, who only loved the mid-century Chinese Communist Party propaganda songs of their youth and didn't care to learn about American rock music. Somehow, the urge to write to a celebrity (and to call D White at that moment a celebrity is a stretch) kept me up at night and wouldn't recede. My imaginary letters often began with *Dear Derrick, you matter to me. Thank you!*

One way I know I am a fan is that I *don't* feel the urge to tell my idol about myself at all. I don't care about him knowing how I grew up, my family life, that I'm a poet, a teacher, the hardship and joys I've experienced, or even the specific things that his determination in basketball has inspired me to do, though these things themselves could fill several dozen letters. Is it the purview of the fan to want to tell their idol about *them*self? It seems a heady mix of selfishness, arrogance, and love that leads us to believe we know something essential about our idols that they don't know themselves. I want him to know that he's a good dad, a good teammate, unusually supportive and willing to sacrifice, a model for attendance and accountability, and that his enthusiasm for shouting out the hard work of parenting is cool. It also matters to me, on a personal level, that he is the kind of dutiful son who would let his Celtics-superfan father tweet relentlessly about his games and give embarrassing father interviews because they seem to bring his father happiness. I often end up calling my parents after games.

The power of love compels me to go on:

When D White shoots a free throw, which goes in 85.4% of the time, he sets his feet and then places his right hand over his heart, takes a deep breath, softly thumps his chest once with an open palm, then shoots. When he misses a shot he either shakes his head so expressively that you can almost hear the *Damn!* while running back up the court, or he claps his hands together once in visible disappointment and apparent self-admonishment or self-encouragement, a distinction he doesn't seem to make. But then, in these moments, D White fans know we are in for something spectacular, because most often after D White misses a shot or commits a turnover, he will chase the ball down on the other end and go up for the most impossibly precise block at the rim you've ever seen. He goes coast to coast in seconds. When asked about it after the game he doesn't deny the cause and effect, that he lost the ball so it was his job to chase it down and try to get a block, as if balancing out his own cosmic scales.

In last year's Eastern Conference finals, after pulling off a miracle last second tip-in to keep the series alive for his team, D White unconvincingly denied crying during the postgame interview. Instead he said, "I'm just happy we won," with a slight crack of amazement in his voice.

He seemed stunned to be embraced with such ferocity by his teammates in the moments after the win, as they shook him and held him to their chests. D White's biggest struggle in the game of basketball is being aggressive, and to be aggressive he needs constant verbal reminders because aggression, even in the sport where he is an elite athlete, in a league where he's been playing for seven years, is uncomfortable to him. When he played in San Antonio, Coach Popovich used to come into the locker room just to find him and say, "Hey. You belong here." D White cites this as the reason why he can now believe that he belongs where he is told he belongs, and when he drops big points in a game he remembers to shout out his teammates for reminding him to be himself.

As a newcomer in fandom, these are the arguably banal factoids about my favorite player that thrill me, and of which I hope I never tire. The pleasure of the fan is in noticing, drawing connections, compiling evidence, judiciously avoiding conspiratorial thinking if possible, doing a kind of relentless analysis that is self-evidently important. Like a chess player, who is like a fan, multiple realities and contingencies must be held open at once depending on what happens in each subsequent possession. A shrug, a grimace, the smirk of a player that has just found their stroke, everything matters. In these ways basketball is the thing that feels the most like *reading* to me, outside of reading. Constantly, the fan is at work considering influence, lineage, the pains of inheritance, who came before who, and begot who, and what style of play, whose character offends who, how many years since X, how many seasons until it will happen again? And who am *I*? What style of play makes me feel most alive? And whose play do I hate, do I find morally repugnant, an insult to the art form? To experience these questions unfold over the course of a game is to notice micro and macro while keeping an eye on the pulsing whole, synthesizing in real time. Readers understand.

Role Playing

Minor players don't get paeans. Sometimes they do, in appropriate relation to a heroic major player in tragedy or death, see: Achilles and his beautiful Patroclus. If there is cause for revelry, it's because they have assisted in the continued majesty and ascension of their star, which they orbit at all times. They were playing their role, and as such are Role Players. A vague and totalizing identity. Much is made of what separates a role player from a star, an amusing binary given that role players are only role players because they aren't stars. The specific criteria are otherwise murky. A mark of morality and congeniality in the NBA is of course to "embrace" being a role player, to humbly sacrifice being a first, second, or third scoring option, to do "the little things that don't show up on the stat sheet," to come off the bench, to lead the second team, etc. It's hard not to love a role player, and it seems true that any serious basketball fan must love several role players, not just stars, or they are not serious about either the sport or their love.

D White, several years on from that *Sportscenter* interview, is a cusp player, a player who receives overtures for being the star of role players, and even more so for being overlooked as the star player he *should* be, which is itself a role-player-cementing logic. There's no role player like the one who deserves better.

In 1989 my parents brought me, aged 2.5, to the United States. We left Beijing for Ithaca, New York, so that my father could study molecular biology at Cornell. In the international and multigenerational phenomenon known as "brain drain," my father played his role quite willingly, to the disappointment of the CCP. We left the country on June 1, three days before the violent events of June 4, 1989, on Tiananmen Square. It was only recently that I learned we stayed in Beijing as a family for several weeks ahead of leaving, experiencing and moving amid the unrest and rising political action. To hear my father tell it, the encampments on the square (echoed so recently by the courageous campus encampments for Palestine around the country, in my telling only), were daily physical impediments to moving around the city for our family. Only this year, 2024, did my father share with me with a certain disaffected quality that he felt intense and direct pressure from friends and classmates to join the encampments and demonstrations on Tiananmen Square, to get out there and be part of what he and everyone else could already sense would be a violent chapter of history. My father says he told friends he supported the encampments, but he just couldn't join them given his family situation and impending departure. How he felt about this refusal, beyond a vague air of resigned "and so it was" attitude, is still opaque to me. He recounts that the situation made transportation in and out of Beijing intentionally difficult, a fact that in the present day I find extremely moving for how it evinces the efficacy and practicality of the student demonstrators. It was, my family's convenience aside, a success of radical disruption.

My father was able to arrange private transportation to the airport, avoiding all public streetcars and subways. In this way, our most crucial prelude to immigration was its own success of privatization. My father also led his professors and professional colleagues to believe that my mother and I were not joining him in the United States, and would instead be waiting patiently for him at home, so as to avoid any suspicion that he and his scientific talents wouldn't be coming back. Even at the airport drop-off, the colleague who had agreed to drive us attempted to usher my mother and I back into the car for the return trip. My father apologized, picked me up, and admitted to him that we were all leaving together. He was sorry to have misled him, and asked for his forgiveness, which according to my father, he got.

After thirty-five years in this country, I felt unprepared to learn that my father had such abiding contact with the events of June 4, that he was so directly entreated to join his peers, that he even considered joining them and then did not, that he defied the surge of radical sentiment coming out of the same universities that had incubated him in order to come to America. When I was young I understood my father was a star of institutional learning, that he had survived every stage of intellectual whittling in order to be offered a fellowship to study in America. I'm not sure I understood just how American we had already become, extricating ourselves from the struggle of others, taking that first step of rugged individualism to ascend (and thus depart to another plane) as stars do. I have felt in the years since, painfully, that my father, in order to survive his choices and his stardom, all that transpired in Beijing following our departure, and the reverberations since then, all such repression and erasure and violence, must have found a way to convincingly tell himself the story where all that followed became simply backdrop, the stage dressing for our Xu family's success. Even history has become the supporting cast for my father's love for his family, or as he calls it, his "total devotion to family." So many of us are these nepotized children of immigration, our fathers or mothers each the stars of their own universe, like mine, the village hero and favorite prodigal son. We all must play our role, and as we agree to rewrite history as they saw it, we do.

A Chip

I won't ever forget the smile, and I choose to imagine that somewhere on the court at TD Garden there remains a small triangle of his tooth pushed through the wax; let it be embedded there forever. D White wears the championship hat and shirt at the ceremony, holding his oldest child in his arms. When it's his turn to speak, and he's called to the microphone, the first command is *Smile for us!*, though he demurs and shakes his head, covers his mouth, looks at his child as if for further permission to deny the request. He is not comfortable, not in this moment when he is temporarily a star, an NBA champion. But a role player always smiles, teeth intact or not. D White says to the crowd, "I'll lose all my teeth for a championship," to raucous applause.

When they replay the footage I can't watch, his face pressed down with such force on the hardwood, putting his fingers immediately to his mouth when he gets up, shaking his head, nodding that something is wrong, he needs a look, the blood and the knowing posture that something bad has happened. For my idol I feel protective, feral, defensive, I wish they wouldn't replay the footage or use it in any montages, don't hurt him, don't try him, don't tease him, don't shame him, don't embarrass him, and most of all don't laugh at him. I am the most parentified fan for him. I think of my father, who has left teeth and more on the company floor, employee of the month more than once, survivor of a three-company merger having taken a devil's bargain to terminate others in exchange for not being terminated. Who went to war for DuPont, Dow Chemical, and whoever else asked, for us; when commanded to *Smile for us!* he did, even when his deeds were ugly and he knew it, so we could continue to love and laud him. Looking at D White on the television I was able to forget for a moment the particularities of this basketball triumph, I thought he must have been pleased that his child saw him smile so wide for the cameras.

When you finish the business, the great Unfinished that has *been* your business for years, what's next? Basketball is a great existential pastime, it confounds as much as it inspires. I won't suggest that it's a great mystery why we get so worked up over athletes putting balls through a net, as sport and competition is human, ancient, genderless. If you begin to care too much about why you care, you're lost in the woods. If you don't care why you care so deeply, perhaps you've achieved some drunken master level of fandom. If you can do this *and* embrace your existential panic at reaching the mountaintop, as all fans hope to do one day, there are unforeseen pleasures ahead. Now that my team has crossed the threshold, I feel a terror and an electric excitement. Will what comes next be disappointing, or majestic? How do I live in the after? Some answers will no doubt come from my father. How to live in this new country of fandom I have chosen?

Paris Book

Why Write? Sick for the Future; Poem on Notre Dame des Champs

June 5

It could be any year, but it's this one. And to it I want to apply a process of attention—this process. My instrument of relation is broken, I feel out of relation with the whole earth, with words I've no occasion to use yet I think about, with other people coming and going shiny and unbothered, maybe a little tired from moving in their slick bodies all day, eating a little ice cream cone that belongs to them in the shade. Am I writing to greet myself once a day? To say hello to what threatens to dissolve into a thin mist if not put to language soon? I'm more than what hurts! I think. Though I'm that, too. I resolve that I will not write, I will log. I won't make something out of nothing.

I still eat bread in the morning, bread throughout the day, cakes at night with whippy frosting, pasta and noodles. I vaguely watch my intake of certain fermentable sugars, when I can remember. My radius of experience is small now, the neighborhood really, occasionally somewhere I can't avoid like the post office. My sports team lost in Game 7. I'm crying about it again. They recovered from a deficit, which you're not supposed to do. They had a miracle of optimism in Game 6 and made us all believe, which you're not supposed to do. A player who is middling and shy and not a star had a star turn of it, a miracle of timing and belief, optimism unleashed. That's really not supposed to happen, and yet it does, all the time. The story they were trying to write is over now. It will have to wait, writing, hoping, it being all the same.

June 6

Delicate little needles placed in my stomach in cross formation, my ankles which tingled a bit, my wrists (green tipped needles), and my feet (red tipped needles). Afterward everything bubbles and gurgles like a baby trying to spit up, and it turns out you do have to treat it like a baby, helpless and scared of the dark.

Went to have sandwiches, nothing remarkable, the perfect white disks of cheese were hypnotic, petri dishes awaiting growth.

Always I am imagining myself in the future, on the airplane, the fear and where it might grip me, expecting those erotic little pings of it. This kind of time travel exists in pockets of wordlessness and nowhere else. If J, bringing words, enters, it dispels. We'll try again tomorrow, as we do.

June 7

Fires up north arrive here, enter our lungs. The sky orange slow-burn, mucus and something else clogs my chest. The something else is big, potentially, and not metaphorical—real heft.

When I discuss poetry and documentation with some students, which I love to do, the students say *truth*, we will have it at any cost! And they are easily willing to turn to themselves with cameras and pens and begin to record and log themselves without worry about audience, language, stakes. They record their meals, emotions, the things said and whispered to them in the fluorescent university café sharing a cinnamon roll, the slights they weather, the disappointments, they record and are proud of their recording. When I ask them, half seriously, to turn "it" into "something" else, they lose interest. As they should. They are given over wholly to the noticing now, and are not interested in abandoning the yet-unnoticed things.

I remind myself too: a record instead of sky, fire, smoke, fatigue.

I step outside to send a message to my sister and parents, describing the color and weight of the ashy light, its quality and my mood, to which they respond, "Oh that's alarming" and then stop responding. Though I know they'll be running to catch up on the news which is somewhere else, not in this text message thread, and possibly I have given it to them too full of feeling. I've done something gross to it without meaning to, something that is writing. I fear I wouldn't go outside today even if the sky and smoke were gone, my body too heavy and full of itself you could say.

June 8

Can I? Is always on my mind. And on other days with further distance: Can she? Probably not.

Earlier I felt something stuck on my eyeball, a plastic fiber, almost invisible were it not slicked in tears and suddenly visible against the membrane of my eye. I plucked it out, wiped it on my pants. No birth to the feeling in my stomach today, another heavy day, mars orange light from the Canadian wilds burning. It wants us dead, lungs full of plastic and ash and fiber.

I can close my eyes and the commercials for antidepressants play just fine on the backs of my eyelids. The bouncing rock is most memorable, losing interest in things it once loved, chasing a butterfly, playing in the rain, strangely moving to me with its slumped shoulders (a rock?) and sad eyes. I read a little bit of *Tropic of Cancer* and wonder if some debauchery wouldn't do the sad rock good, a little bit of forced eroticism for mental health. Or would that just add to its stack of ills. When J says he loves me it makes me want to never write again.

In the summer of 2012 I began a journal in Massachusetts, wanting to record The Loneliest Summer, and the way I set about preserving my loneliness then was to agree to do things and then cancel at the last minute. It became known that I had a dislike for doing things, when I actually had wanted to do all the things I didn't do, I was just afraid, and I hadn't yet realized that I was always afraid. That summer, writing and fear began to twist up with each other in strange ways such that I was sure I needed to be afraid to write. And so I was, and I did.

I'd like to know when exactly I became afraid, and if my belief about my mother's fear being the genesis of my fear is accurate in a larger way than what's self-evident. She always did tell me that everything was to be feared. But for a period of time after childhood, and before real adulthood, it was like I stopped being able to hear her. Were those the good old days? When I wasn't really my mother's child.

June 9

Only sometimes does feeding myself not feel alien, repellant. It felt good to walk, to churn myself on two legs to the pharmacy, back home with the toilet paper, to kiss J on his cheek and give him his medicine, to leave him at the desk to work a little while longer on *La Cavaliere*, by Nathalie Quintane, which he is translating, which I haven't been allowed to read yet. Some days I can't put it down, the heavy gloom, and instead I set the facts of the day into orbit around it, so that it may remain the center of my world, but not impede the day's motion around it.

June 10

This depression says to me *leave society*. But I realize my desire to leave society and reappear (intact, corporeal, well) in some other place is strong, while my desire to cease to exist is weak. Maybe that's love calling to me, keeping me.

June 11

June 12

June 13

Not many words.

June 21

Paris, it's an embarrassment to be here. Undeserved. Where the birds are nesting. A sense of my body filled often with air, enormous empty space. What should be blowing instead in a curtain, romantic and slow, instead bloats from the inside without consent, giving me more of myself to carry. Walking around I have this feeling like I want to laugh at myself with someone, a total stranger, but there is just more of myself, and so my own laughter floats out and sags in the air, sort of sad and self-critical, not like laughter at all. In the evening, singing outside. And summer solstice.

June 25

Let me try again, with real effort, to send this news to the future:

On that first day, June 19, I had taken several kinds of sedatives, some medicine for stomach upset, an anxiety pill, and had fasted for about fourteen hours, so was able to stroll down the Boulevard Montparnasse that appeared before me, seeing Paris for the first time, relatively unbothered with interest enough to stop in a noodle shop and patiently watch them hand-pull the dough. Two French couples at our table struck up a conversation with each other, Oh it's so hot, Oh I know! We should have thought twice about sitting in the sun. Tinkling laughter. One couple was old, one was young. I suppose J and I were American. The sun moved undiscerningly into all of our faces while we ate our noodles, mine topped with little shrimp that for some reason I thought of as *dead shrimps.*

I fell asleep in the afternoon, woke up sometime between 3:00 p.m. and 8:00 p.m. and went out for another walk, made it as far as the Monoprix (far) instead of Monoprix (close) and even took the long way back, looked at labels for peanut butter in disbelief that peanut butter exists away from home, though it's thinner and creamier. Ate tinned fish, bread, salad on the balcony at last, saw the view and took some photos for nobody. The sensation I had was of being very far away from everything important. We congratulated ourselves on not falling asleep before midnight.

On the second day I slept late, ate little, felt sharp and dull alternating aches in my pelvis and went straight back to bed, was it the food or lack of it, something about this new place or something brought over from the old? I had wanted to walk to the Jardin du Luxembourg and could not, too "laid up" as they say, throttled less by pain than by fear of pain, equally bright in the center of my body. I ate one large pill of supposedly living bacteria which were to slowly (over time, if I were diligent enough) colonize my small intestine with their benevolence and create a more efficient digestion. I would one day eat comfortably, so I could dream. I would feed and grow myself without pain again.

I took more painkillers, dressed myself, and walked two blocks to Le Select to sit outside and watch people go by on the sidewalk, thinking they were not also looking at me. When J stood up and went inside to use the restroom, I counted up the seconds until he returned, with the thought that if I were to need to leave before he returned I would not be able to, because the coffee J had ordered had not yet been paid for, and thus I would either have to leave without paying, or speak with the waiter to pay for J's coffee. I was unsure how to draw the attention of the waiter in this case and how to proceed with payment. I also worried that if J came back to find me gone he would worry, understandably, and not know where to look for me first, if he should go home or look around on the street in case someone had come and taken me. I was not taken nor did my panic rise to such a level, J returned, and we left together.

I noticed that it was very popular to order the seafood tower, which is well described by its name. The clams and shrimp and other shellfish are displayed right on the sidewalk in cold bins with a small drainage pipe beneath, and a waiter floats by to extract as many pieces of assorted seafood as you've ordered straight onto the tray and onto your table. The large clams were looking slightly under-cooled, their bin nearly empty of ice while the other compartments had been replenished with more ice chips heaped on top, and I found that this preoccupied me (who ate the large clams, how many) for much of the evening.

On the fourth day I felt an unease between the lower two ribs, something needling beneath. But it was beautiful there in the garden, and slow, and it had space for me, more importantly time, precious, real. I stayed. I had the urge again to find somebody, two somebodies would also do, that could witness my existence now in the garden, my miraculous appearance, narcissistically Christlike to myself, ideally somebody or somebodies who had also seen me convalescing in my apartment the day before, unable to come out as I had now come out, to see my overcoming. Maybe these two somebodies were themselves foreigners in Paris, but for whom entering public space was no trouble at all, to walk forth from a known place, the Jardin to the Pantheon to the shaded half-wall in tribute to the dead, to the Seine, to the magical sub-ground toilets that abut Notre Dame half-reconstructed and still wearing its dressing gown, to the teenagers down by the milky green water, the boat with the Sun Wu Kong pathfinder, the drunk Americans dancing inside with doubles of each other. Might these two see me and pat me, on the shoulder as my parents once did, pat pat pat, there you are, don't cry. You exist.

At the water for the first time that day I would not cross. Not for anything or anyone.

June 27

No, none.

July 6

There was for whatever reason the following autobiographical poem to write today. It eased something small and sharp in my brain, despite my wanting to refuse it.

POEM ON NOTRE DAME DES CHAMPS

A pigeon named Daddy visits us these days
His skull devoid of language, in an elegant "V"

In the summer words don't come when they're called
They *surface* lazy, they float

Don't cry! We told the crying child, it's making us hate you
It's making us hate ourselves

Imagine instead that you are in the air and beneath you
is the Seine, a river famous for appearing insidiously green

in the imagination of more than 1 lunatic poet at a time
As you walk, thoughts puffing, palms flexing

A glow begins to orbit your head instead of grief
You ask him, Babe, did you have a nice time at the library?

I wish I hadn't been that crying child
I wish I wasn't here now, separated from her, watching

a cop deploy his military shield against the air
Doing a little two-step

There should be a word just for him, seeing him
A grotesque guttural sound that sends him directly to hell

Little passageways open in the word, spells for death
When I wake up I've forgotten which way to the Jardin du Luxembourg

It hurts to be filled with so much expectation
Now let us explore how poetry is made

July 9

Expository urges only appear when other urges are muted—I wonder if this is true for all writers. I don't think I hope it's true. Urges for poetry, for food, for rest, for sex, for speech. My expository dimness is now embarrassing. I'm not sure what there is to say about anything. I go out now, every day, without missing a day, like never before. I long to be out, out of bed, to be in it, to be a little bit afraid of it as I'm sitting excitedly in the moment, the present, in the shade of the oaks on the northwest side of the Jardin which I like best, eating bread and tomatoes, to talk with J and be a little nervous from happiness, like a bug biting flesh, or small children riding horses in a loop led by their mothers.

Today I'll allow one line, a true one: green parrots in the trees, six gooselings in the grass.

When I call my father on the phone he says, "Ah, that's the real stuff!" about travel.

July 16

Illness, J and I both, everything smell-less and tasteless, a totally beige and smooth surface to experience, weird, not erotic, just a blank of sensation. As if to revive sensation I dive into my phone's screen too much, I want to look at anything else instead but it sucks me in, taking and needing and giving fear, buying and shaming, the place where pain and money come together. Expository urge returns, haha. As my body has been inside for an entire week now, other urges diminished.

"I will begin on the Paris book now" and he does, Henry Miller. What would I do with a Paris book anyway? I was supposed to rest this summer, to rest and be with others, not with more of myself or my book. The Paris Book should not exist and if ever it does I will have failed. I'll come back tomorrow to denigrate the Paris Book more. I miss the birds. Last night watching *All Quiet on the Western Front*, war's demonic logic, the film was magnificent and I sobbed on the balcony where I was keeping my distance from J. The Paris Book could be my private joke.

Aug 11

Days slow and accelerate at will, which is not ours, some other things' will entirely, not human or plant, something else. A month has come and gone, between this and thoughts of the Paris Book. And thank god it did not come to pass, not that it was really in danger of appearing, but it has obediently kept itself away. Does that mean I have succeeded to rest, in exile from writing? Did I do it, get away from myself? I'm not sure that I have, though I have slowly floated through more days than one can hold in one's mind without blurring. That's something. Days that slip out of the fist.

Where have I been? Many places and even across the river, not many times but I did exist on the right bank once or twice. Once to buy our rings for each other, J and I. Then I was on the left bank alone, J traveled to Germany, taking myself along the narrow new path that curves behind the ugly gash of highway, a dumb behemoth curve that you duck under, cutting up the face of Paris in such a nasty way. Just before it denies you to cross you'll be at the Museé Bourdelle, just there on the right, where I was told admission was free and wandered the gardens and ceiling-height marble statues feeling small, looking up at the bellies of horses riding into battle, poor things, feeling a buzzing inside me as the air shifted itself around my organs, the air trapped and swirling which has been my companion all these weeks. I stayed, despite myself. I saw the "faces of horror" that Bourdelle sculpted of the soldiers, in the narrow hallway displayed in a row, the twisted mouths and lumpy heads, teeth angry and wild, with a placard asking children to consider the faces, the depiction, and then to answer for themselves: "How do you think Bourdelle felt about war?"

A feeling later that I would go on living, then. At least to peer around the next corner, to tomorrow. To see if my news does indeed reach myself there.

The urge pushes here to predict how it will go, the final length of days, about six, before a return. But no. Ça suffit.

What I Don't Know About '89

Meeting My Baba in Poetry

There is so much known to others, but unknown to me, that it seems both arrogant and profound (the writer's special blend) to want to know what nobody knows. To start there, and not with the humbler act of receiving known knowledge. And yet.

One way a writer turns unknowing into knowing is by listing out all the things she doesn't know that are critical to her life. I am describing fiction. I thought to write a list of things including facts, names, consequences, locations, secrets, etc., that I don't know about the events of June 4, 1989, on Tiananmen Square, some of which others know and some of which is unknown to all, but all of which is critical to the writing of a novel about Tiananmen Square which I have somehow set out to do.

What I don't know, after investigating if it is known to others, I must imagine, and what I imagine I inevitably misrepresent, which I hope will not feed that writer's tendency, against all good intention, of aestheticized unknowing. How else to do this work of writing a past that I did not live?

It's not within the genre of fiction that I've done the most thinking about this problem, but rather in the genre that often precedes the writing of fiction: the genre of statements requesting institutional support and money for one's potential writing. This genre seems duly, and consistently, to run on value judgments around credibility, belief, preparation, and talent, all of which must be conveyed via writing that is the opposite of writing that interests me. But despite reluctance, I've cultivated some interest in the writing that requests support for the writing of a novel that doesn't exist, and about which not much is known. The many degrees of "speculative" that make up this writing interest me.

I often begin by declaring, in this most speculative of speculative genres, that my writing is informed greatly (with a caveat for not exclusively) by my own immigration and the tight-knit community of Chinese American immigrants that raised me in the Midwestern United States. This is another way of admitting that what I hope to depict, I did not live, and thus I cannot be my own primary source. I am filled up with the generative possibilities of un-knowing, I mean to say. Truly, it spills over. Among other unknowns,

- What the air was doing that day, how the dense unmovable smog of Beijing, the smog that turned the inside of my nose coal-black after only a half-day playing outside with my grandfather, affected the breathing of thousands of souls gathered in one place shouting and inhaling with such force.
- How my father felt on a scale of shame to freedom, which only he can know, leaving all that history behind.
- What is the psychic burden of '89 *really* and how does it manifest in the generation born that same decade, many of whom came of age in Western countries in the shadow of an unknowable event.
- If the silence around it is a wound or a balm.
- Does it deserve folkloric significance, does it create any meaningful wisdom concerning history, resentment, assimilation, political obedience.
- How *do* you behave in order to survive a government.
- What it looked like from the airplane, our once-in-a-lifetime god's eye view if you can call it that, what two immigrants and a baby could hope to see while up there in god's living room. If it was blue and green like a globe, water and jade, a blue eyeball and a well-watered lawn.
- If anything else meaningful can be said after Xiaobo's *June Fourth Elegies*; if anything should.

I was raised by a reader, my Baba, who finds little use in not-knowing, and prefers instead to quickly *know* by gathering up the Wikipedia-style facts of a subject and filling in the rest with rhetorical flourishes that make it appear as if his knowing began a long time ago. My Baba is a reader who should have been an artist, a writer, and a teacher (as he came to wish later in life), who became a biologist instead.

Often when I talk to my Baba about one topic I imagine we are actually talking about another topic, '89, and that through these talks my Baba is imparting to me both his political and emotional beliefs through allusion and projection about that which we both can't directly talk. For example if my Baba and I talk about the popularity of lab-grown meats, which he finds to be "interesting" but not interesting enough to eat or invest money in, I also come to understand that my Baba is trying to caution me away from trendification and the ephemeral "fads" that sweep through a generation only to abandon that generation without fulfilling any of its utopian promises. My Baba implies that an unwise person who is also impatient would invest in something like synthetic meat, only to be disappointed and potentially even bankrupted by the inevitable collapse of its societal promise. While we are talking about lab-grown meats, my Baba speaks with a resentment-tinged ferocity that feels disproportionate to the stakes of the conversation, leading me to believe that he is also latently speaking about revolutionary tides, the ebbs and flows of which are to be ridden out. In fact it seems to me that anytime my Baba and I speak about anything touching the future, or faith, optimism, risk, violence, or privacy, I am filling in another hole of my unknowing.

Recently I spent a semester living near my Baba for the first time since moving out of his house to attend college, and was able to spend more time soliciting his opinions on topics including:

Vein size as one ages
The resurrection of Christ (accuracy)
Gene-sequencing technology (ethics)
Whether sending a letter across a long distance is inherently romantic
Is genre real?
Speeding tickets
Baba's problem with forgetting to wear his seatbelt (death drive)
AI dupes (mechanical Turks)
Lunar New Year traditions
The unplucked brow of Pasolini's Christ

On this last topic, my Baba had a lot of opinions, most of them critical. Pier Paolo Pasolini's *The Gospel According to St. Matthew* (1964) depicts the life of Christ from birth up through the crucifixion and resurrection, hitting most of the canonical scenes from Christ's life like the healing of the lepers, the betrayal by Judas, etc. You could say that Pasolini hews close to the text, and includes the biographical chapters known to believers and nonbelievers alike. Christ's Greatest Hits. It was this film that I watched with him one evening after dinner.

Throughout, Christ is played viscerally and often agonizingly by Enrique Irasoqui, a Spanish economics student who had never acted before, which Pasolini apparently preferred in the spirit of Italian neorealism.[1] This Christ is also decidedly human, without hint of glamour, not ideal, certainly not muscular or virile or sexual, somewhat androgynous as real human bodies are when freed from performing gender. This Christ is thin and looks appropriately hungry, dirty, tired, and stooped, a Christ whose body carries the marks of his wandering. His gaze is more sad than it is kind. Pasolini's movie ends with Christ's iconic resurrection, his Protagonist Energy moment whereby death is shaken off and the emptiness of the tomb announces his return.

For my Baba and Mama, this important cinematic moment was botched by Pasolini, adding insult to injury after the film-long sin of Christ's overall physical unattractiveness. Christ should be perfect, majestic, virile above all, a fulfillment of the image of his heavenly father and not a depiction of the human man under whose name he temporarily lived and died. Instead Pasolini's Christ returns unspectacularly, underwhelmingly, which is to say humanly: the tomb is discovered to be empty; an angel informs the visitors that Christ has risen and has gone ahead of them to Galilee, that they will find him there. He appears one last time, still plainly clothed, for a few final seconds of the film, standing on an ordinary rocky hillside, speaking to the disciples of his authority in heaven and earth.

As much as the New Testament emphasizes and perhaps even hinges on Christ's human years being filled with all those most human things (work, suffering, fatigue, hunger, wandering, loneliness, worry), my Baba seemed to find it horrifying that Christ would have a prominent unibrow on screen when the option to not have one was readily available. In the scene that precedes the crucifixion, where Christ wanders the wilderness ahead of his capture, he calls out achingly to his father in despair, his brow covered with unseemly sweat, the agony of his body writhing with heat, emotional pain, and the foresight of a man who knows that his own death comes next. Movingly (in my opinion only), Pasolini chooses to frame Christ in this scene from above, emphasizing the derangement of his body and its posture of defeat, poverty, and emotional devastation.

Here, too, I am trying to learn about the things that my parents will not talk to me about through the things that they will. Their palpable disappointment in Pasolini's poetic and visceral treatment of Christ's life is not that it was shown to be a human life, but that Pasolini deprives Christ of his godlike return, the transcendence of his human suffering which evinces the necessity of the suffering. For Christ not to arrive, visually, into splendor and glamour, to be transformed from person to image, was difficult for my parents to accept, as if Pasolini had stripped Christ of some of his final dignity and rendered his sacrifice moot.

If my Baba has an ideology about the visual language of suffering, the requirements for protagonism and narrative, does he not have a poetics? I don't believe he sees himself as Christlike, at least not more than the principle to *behave* with Christlike mercy compels any Christian, but he does relate to sacrifice in particular, how it heightens achievement, and how an immigrant must choose to believe that it is a promise, not a risk. My Baba is *prodigal* in many ways, the only son out of six children born in a small farming village in Shandong, China, the only one to leave the country which ensures that he returns to fanfare each time. That it would be intolerable to him to return, after sacrifice, to anything less than an ecstatic celebration of his protagonism, makes sense to me.

One of poetry's pleasures is the permission to draw one's credibility from many realms of experience. I don't articulate this as a distinction that excludes other genres, only that I find it to be a quality amplified in poetry. Writing *of* is one option, which for the poet may give way to writing from, through, around, even writing fully avoidantly, in the enormous shape of the void of *it*, paying careful attention to trace the contours accurately, revealing the emotional boundary lines of loss. In this way poetry is perfect for the writer who does not know, who is called to write with such great unknowing. And how does the poet credentialize herself? Is it untrue to say it's with feeling? Certainly in more ways than with suffering or a pound of flesh—the poem doesn't require that of us, though it seems able to hold what suffering needs to be held.

My Baba and I are lucky, we meet each other in poetry. From a reader of poems at a young age, my Baba has become a writer of them, prolific and devoted. He continues to tell me about what he won't write through what he will, challenging me to parse and surmise subtext and give thanks for exactly how my life as a poet has prepared me for this pleasure of close-reading him. What we don't know about each other, be they secrets or stories lost to time, we have often learned in this meeting place. What we won't say to each other appears here too. I can imagine, with a laugh, someone telling my Baba that this country of poetry is not his to enter, that the path paved by his sacrifices was for his daughter to walk alone. Never mind if she would rather walk it with her Baba at her side.

My favorite poem by my Baba is entitled "Winter Day," written in 2023. For at least the past five years my Baba's poems have come steadily, often dropped into our family's group chat without much fanfare. Sometimes, he will write, "please enjoy my new poem," but never "please tell me what you think." "Winter Day" was written after a heavy snow in Iowa, where he lives, a few days before Christmas. To over-read my Baba is a risk I must now take, for his role as my Baba forbids him from ever being my friend, or making the kinds of disclosures one makes to a friend. He rarely speaks to me from personal vulnerability or emotional need, never despair, and always with room to hold *my* pain or sorrow. My Baba would never ask me to carry him. He sent the poem without preface to the family chat in the early evening, followed by a short message wishing me a great Christmas, since I would be unable to spend it with him that year. The poem, thus tied to the distance between us, can't escape it.

"Winter Day" is five couplets, each couplet ending in a rhyme except for the last couplet, which doesn't rhyme even a little bit. It appears below in entirety, with my Baba's permission:

WINTER DAY

On this cold and gloomy winter day,
Loneliness grows, an unwavering sway.

Snowflakes gently drift and play,
Evoking a boundless love, I must say.

Wandering the long street, I wrap my concerns tight,
To thwart the encroaching melancholy's might.

From afar, a piano melody Fur Elise does chime,
Instantly, my troubles dissolve in its rhyme.

I quicken my pace toward my home,
Bestow upon myself a warm smile.[2]

I love how the precociously unrhyming last word of the poem, "smile," breaks something so formal as it bestows itself upon the speaker. Cleverly, the couplet preceding ends with "my troubles dissolve in its rhyme," referring to the tune of "Für Elise" (my Baba's favorite) but perhaps also to the scaffolding of the poem itself. Freed now from rhyme, the poem must end, the speaker must quicken toward home.

My Baba would never speak of his personal loneliness, at least not in a manner that would concern his children, yet here it is spoken of freely, growing even, "an unwavering sway." I'm charmed by the following image of playful snowflakes, unbothered and sweet, having some nullifying effect on the swelling gloom that the speaker feels. I choose to read the phrase "I must say" with an emphasis on the *must*, rather than on the phrase itself as three filler syllables to complete a rhyme. "I must say," monosyllabic and declarative of its own needfulness, evinces its own necessity as the poet's charge. I read my Baba as making an existential declaration here, and an ars poetica.

But the speaker wanders and struggles on. At this point in my Baba's poetry writing, I know he is using "long street" metaphorically, just as he now uses the figurative image of concerns as a too-thin overcoat, insufficient to protect the speaker. You must believe that to me, it was nearly explosive to read a first-person poem by my Baba speaking on melancholy, loneliness, and the long road on which one must struggle. "Für Elise" is a melody from my Baba's youth, one that never fails to transport him back in time, so for it to "instantly" dissolve the speaker's troubles seems right. This incites the hurrying home, toward family and familiarity.

The final line of the poem is its best and most subtly surreal. "Bestow upon myself a warm smile" is logistically strange, nearly an image of dissociation, and intentionally grandiose in the verb of "bestow." There is somehow a self that looks and smiles upon another self here. The song and the smile are either a comically tidy conclusion to inner turmoil or a fairly devastating resignation—a consolation. What draws the speaker home with urgency after all? Is it comfort, or duty? Responsibility may call, the same responsibility that incites loneliness? A warm smile, given by nobody, will have to suffice, it seems. Is it a final image of restraint or release? Not knowing is part of this final line's knotty and moving pleasure. Even the "boundless love" cited earlier in the poem, evoked by snowflakes, seems to appear in the poem with such initial emotional heft only to quickly recede. Which kind of ephemeral boundless love is this, and from what realms familial, cultural, religious, parental, or spiritual, does it emanate?

From my Baba's poetry I have learned about knowledge and ignorance, and in this way (among others) anything I dare to write drawn from the unknown will be tribute to him. A more recent poem that I love, from 2024, entitled "Seeking and Visiting Plum Blossoms in the Snow" narrates a "perilous journey" through the deep winter snow to see the Goddess of Plum Blossoms, beautiful, noble, "blossoming wildly under the sky filled with flying snowflakes." It's a sensual and melancholy poem, turning from a vision of ecstatic beauty and poetic inspiration toward the final line, "Urging onward on the journey through the years."[3] Weariness, by premonition, rules the end of the poem, and the muse of flowers can only serve as a fading memory, ghostlike. Knowledge compels yet fades, leaving behind the absence where my Baba and I meet again.

Notes for an Opening (2015–2020)

Time is very interesting in an academic sense
In a lived sense it is the most boring thing in the world
What do I observe, internalize, "move on" from, regret, jest at, forgive,
invite?
My family gathers in the courtyard without me
They scrutinize my usage of the language I labored to acquire
"I hate to lose" is what I say to the Bank of America fraud consultant

I wanted to craft a more outstanding mode of engagement with the soul
To get children to finish their dinners say "children in Asia are starving"
Is more like "at points my family has been starving"
I relate to my friend that third world factory work is not an abstraction
My family name has held the position for years
•
When the Foxconn worker commits suicide a catalog of his poetry is
released online[1]
He describes a moon made of iron, a nail he swallows
It unsettles me because he is many people that I know, except they are
not yet dead
He is not an abstraction
When I describe this to my friend, my friend is intensely interested in
applying pressure to the context of the poems' writing, how much the
tragedy skews our appreciation of the craft of the poems themselves
I am unable to see how it is not all the poem
I begin to feel trapped inside the tower of white western intellectual
consideration
I feel sick, and worse, "misunderstood"
•

I don't want to be called the other female Chinese poet's name anymore
Or if I am mistaken for the other female Chinese poet, I want a long apology in the moment of the recognition of the mistake
What I resent most is the punitive sensibility this is breeding inside me

•

Hunger for some immunity against desire
Which is in itself a ferocious desire replicating itself across screens
My desire is to achieve, produce, consume, succeed
My desire perhaps is to be regarded while I undertake this process over time

Fear of the loss of my white allies
Or is it, fear of my white allies

•

I have long fantasized about writing a book called The View From Here
People talk about the human condition as infinitely stable
The view from the present condition
I find myself respecting others up to the threshold at which I personally begin to suffer
Infinitely separated from them in the moment of our supposed unity, bearing witness to spontaneous acts of nature (bay, dolphins) or mutual disaster (lost phone)
I do not like crowds, mandatory participation, enclosed spaces
Time is absolutely boring and violent

•

And yet often: so regrettably heartbroken over "things as they are"
Wait for life as it happens
I might revise this in the morning, effected by the various metaphors of weather
When the violin cries, reaches out toward an unsustainable note
I often worry over seeming clever or unfeeling
I feel repelled by the present moment
A violation of my religious and spiritual beliefs which dictate a present mind

Enter: an evaluation of this text as poetry
Immediately some distance is expanded, the text leans away

Mostly I aspire to an authentic record of thinking situated firmly in time and space
A caveat for the meaninglessness of authenticity, its evaluative impossibilities

•

I go down to the store for replacement bread
They do not have the bread I like, I return home

A primal selfishness leads me to record this in writing
I too seek the femininity of the open page
You love to exist in the historical moment, there beneath the red "Pepsi Cola" sign
Corporations aspiring to humanity
I lingered to speak with her in my native language
Sociolinguistically it is not my native language
Considerations of: what is my "native" language
The question of where and among whom do I feel most unabashedly myself
That is, where am I most contrasted with others?
An immigrant dreams of total assimilation as both fantasy and nightmare
The abstraction of my self-remembrance

•

Evaluation is so boring and relates thus to time

•

On June 1, 1989, I was a baby carried on an airplane away from Shandong, China, the place of my birth, and it was later related to me that during the flight I exhibited supernatural calm, a sense of devotion (submission) to the isolation I would later experience
I have mythologized it to the point of memory
Golf masters do this, alongside prisoners of war: intense visualization over time seems to the body as good as lived experience
The imagination is an abstraction
Three days later protestors are massacred in Tiananmen Square and the irony of the name of the place seems too cheeky, too perfect to talk about
"The Gate of Heavenly Peace"

My father participated quite fully in "brain drain"
In my adult life I throw up on public transportation
I write "false correlation" on the board and slash it red
Adults at the time say there was something in the air and mean it as fully abstract though it is fully literal
What was in the air?

•

The face of the Foxconn worker haunts me in its eerie resemblance to my father's
This depresses me
Have you ever put cucumbers in your water? It tastes exactly the same
You open the document
You highlight what is disagreeable in red, you cut it from the page
You make no incision
You agree strongly with the content but not with the manner of its dissemination
The joke of it was how much it cost and this translation into hours labored

•

Impossible then to locate the burial site of feelings within the body
Nor am I convinced that the seductiveness of reverence for the body is productive
Nonetheless I give myself over to it
Nonetheless I see in you such "material potential"
Some words here from the speaker last night: your goals for me are oppressive
The roses outside were all pink slumped over in a bucket where I regard them and take their picture
What is recorded, how they once were, might have been

Where you cut it, it grows there double
Where you splice the tender shoot sprouts (in its exact location) a twinning of branches
This is so beautiful and nonhuman I don't know what to say

•

When I loved you deeply and with abandon I saw you without humanity, as an object turning in place

Thus I may replace, regard, dissolve you
A process of welcome retrograde
A process of my own doubt enacted on the living stage of the real
Could I have related to you better as an "artificial intelligence"

•

Or do I hear, a factory outside
Or do I hear, a family outside

•

Who eats whom
Under which flag?

or

Do not describe any more things to me as "ancient"
You are not allowed beyond the stone and the wall, the courtyard
And what is beyond it
The snow was coming down beyond outside the window, beneath the sky
Perhaps I wanted to know you prepositionally

How and toward whom can I relate if by relation I diminish myself
I obsess over the problem of space
It is not that necessarily you oppress me, rather that I have come to know myself only ever in relation to you and our relationship is historical
Let there be no visual representation of me without you
Adjust my gaze so that I may be warm enough to please you

•

In a painting: white is the prelude smeared over several figures
I roll an old apple between my hands feeling its rot
What else can I describe within the verbal framework "in today's world"
Who is still living in "yesterday's world?"
And who is their president
And what technologies drive their daily operations in the snow-globe of the past

When he attributes to me an unfounded Eastern heritage of *naturalism* I ball my fists

Am I a child now and if so who is coming to bring me home

My mother sews your mother's beautiful dresses by hand

I'm not mad about it

I just wanted you to know

•

To honor my mother: "be twice as good as them to be taken half as seriously"
She was pinning up her dark hair with a blue jewel
I was a child maybe, or I was still bloating up with life inside of her
Here I wish to continue being sentimental and wonder about the limits of your suspension of disbelief
No, your suspension of suspicion at my remembrance
Could it be dripping of elegy
Does it violate our contract whereby I approach you as one would a priority

Do you still feel our friendship opening like an exquisite pink blossom?

Are you uncomfortable and if so, why?

•

In the dream last night I was desperately arranging cut flowers for something important
The practical uses of my work I was not made aware
Nobody was available to assist
Thus the flowers were strewn around the carpet beside me
I was compelled to finish my task by something greater than myself
The forces that acted upon me seemed to say, "Your life depends upon this assemblage"
I took it as a warning, though provocative, though urgent and abstract
The bouquets were to be picked up as soon as I made the call
I admit, it felt good to be the lone member of mission control
There's no point in talking of how time passes in a dream; I worked for minutes
Perhaps I worked for years

The only accompanying sound was a song looping in my mind about a
  little sparrow
A Chinese folk song from somewhere, the past
I was so alone in my freedom to choose, but because I was under
  deadline, a duress
I did not dare make a mistake
After some time, I stepped away from my work and admired the results
The outcome was beautiful, and because I had worked very hard: *rare*

•

We don't remember how we got here, so have woven a beautiful story of
  replacement
You mispronounce my sacred name, always in front of others, there it
  goes
A fine white mist where once it held space for me
I didn't write for the longest time because you were speaking for me
You had so many eyes trained on you, I wanted them only on me
In order for me to work toward an undoing of my condition, I must
  know the characteristics of my condition
In order for me to know the characteristics of my condition, I must not
  be made to feel alone in my perception of them
You are and have always been subject to randomness
Accept it

•

In World War II the chemical giants (Monsanto, DuPont) made a fortune
  through exclusive government contracts to spray death from above
If you think about it for too long you will feel hysterical
You will point erratically at the audience in a frenzied state
You will stare at the miniature hurricane of Liquid Plumber spiraling
  down toward the clog like a heavy godsend

•

Poems of the deadpan subject
Poems of the habitually deferred
Poems of the yellow hand and matching face
Poems of the song that feels like a secret
Poems of the fancy free
Poems of the who and what do I love now with all this money?

•

I had felt the similes falling away from my holy body
In sharp relief and judgment of you, who have yet to recognize me
I wanted disgusting excess for my family this year, my food out of your mouth
But my practice was of looking at the image and conjuring it up from the margins
I was crying there in the great hall like something I had never felt
It was repugnant to words
You had your eyes trained on me crying in church
I was tired of being worn by you like fashion and hungry for my life to begin
I attempted to face the successes of those around me

•

Pedestrian thoughts again about the body in recovery
Fragile clock, weak and porous until suddenly in revolt
All these days stuck alone at home
Parents in the world are like a roving evaluation, never knowing where their gaze will fall
On the mouse emerging from the wall
On the wall itself, in need of repair
A friend says, "My accent never fails to make them laugh" and I catch myself laughing
Then laugh again at the brilliant entrapment
The completion of a closed unintentional loop
Lost to laughter now, unable to suck it back into my body
I read a testimony about the loneliness of large unfilled spaces and sense my parents preparing to board the plane now

•

Your historical loveliness knows no bounds
Urging and seething in its own image across time, a discontent of form
A self muting (or is it mutilating) lexicon
Who is Tank Man to you?
Tank Man torn apart by my would-be friends
Tank man dancing immortal as GIF
Tank Man as where you stop reading
Tank Man has been around the world but not back
Tank Man as nobody you care to know

I left and I admit I did not turn around, how could I, I was still shitting in my diaper
Every June I look around and you are ordering Tank Man, I am reunited with him on your plate
The day passes over you with grease on its wings
It was a luxurious silence, then a long sleep in the margins where my family owns a plot
Things as they are *are* inexorable
Time felt absolute and came back to humiliate me
I acknowledged language, my untrustworthy friend
A consideration of my new home was anatomical and of many parts I was ashamed
Filled with an abstract grief
Tank Man doesn't care about your velveteen ideas of protest
Tank Man finally on vacation on Martha's Vineyard
Tank Man declining to be killed by you just a few more times
Tank Man as a cosmology of fetishized suffering at the center of the world
I had said to people "Is it funny"
If I am a social animal, I say much more or much less

•

Last night on the phone, bored to death while Dad live-translates my new poems into Chinese
He probes the meaning behind phrases until I think, "You just don't get it"
Later he explains to me the metrics of Chinese classical verse and I think, "I just don't get it," and we laugh together
A sound not unlike a bell
It is beautiful to please one's parents
Though somewhere it is written that piety is neither interesting nor progressive

•

Mom tells me a story: an immigrant arrives *here*
Eventually working second shift at a garment factory she saves up enough money to purchase a used car
Then she must take a driving test, then she must secure childcare to travel to the test but cannot afford it

She asks to bring her baby in the car and is granted permission
She is nervous and immediately places the car in reverse
Nearly fails then and there
The roads are covered with ice and you must imagine a brutal winter
It is dangerous for Mom and baby both
Who then, is at fault?
If your flight lands at JFK but the shuttle leaves from LaGuardia
And you must take a bus with your four rolling suitcases and baby
It's not that you are afraid, but something entirely more particular
An ache that moves frequently and with greater purpose

•

Flowers carried on an invisible hand above the ocean, color peeling off
 of me
Ruled by Chinese astrology, which is to say mood, I eat the mooncake to
 prepare for the new year
My sadness supplements my vision when I write
A factory where I reproduce myself daily, go nonverbal
Like beach trash and unanswered questions

•

Suppose I oppose the corporate merger of DuPont and Dow Chemical
After the merger, the mega company will be re-split into three new
 entities
One for textiles, one for chemicals, one for agriculture
The third of which employs not one but both of my parents
The layoffs are imminent and the mood in the office is tense
Dad missed his opportunity to transition laterally into academia and we
 are all nervous
Dad has acquired numerous bio-patents over the years, the prestige of
 which will likely allow him to keep his job
He appears in the diversity initiative videos produced by the company
He brings them home on a little flash drive
I pull a knife across the grapefruit's glistening skin and can't bear to
 watch

•

Admit: that moment in time is completely imaginary
You do not remember nor can you ever
You call it up into being at will

Perhaps we did not even travel to the airport in any kind of hurry or under duress
Perhaps we stopped for lunch in the wide public square
Mom admired the perfectly manicured azaleas, the trim shrubbery
Crowds violently dispersed only to reassemble at different points in the city
Traffic must have been very bad, though we might have bypassed it all by taking the subway all the way to the terminal
Or the train on its reliable tracks
Admit it again: that moment in time is completely imaginary
If we cried, it's difficult to say what we mourned the loss of
There was so much we would not see again for many years
Did we pass through any checkpoints on the way?
Was Dad questioned for his timely departure from the country?
Did they ask him what he studied in Beijing, who he consorted with, his political views?
Do you support a democratic upheaval now or have you ever?
Why are you leaving today?
By design or by luck we boarded the plane
I didn't cry once, the sweetest baby on an international flight the others had ever seen
Perhaps I became the star of the trip, passengers cooed over my impressive calm
Perhaps Mom and Dad cried in lieu of me
I had not yet known about my losing

•

A wish list:
You who have listed me first
You who follow
You who name me incorrectly
You who do nothing to find me
"You and Yours"
You who would bring up the rear
Your friends
Your enemies
You who would mispronounce me
You especially, saying nothing

•

Yesterday all I managed to write was a note to myself that read, "what is
this poem even about," and unable to find the poem in question
In the nineties my parents took what jobs they could get
With each paycheck we felt our loneliness coming to an end
Pointless cut flowers began to appear next to the kitchen sink
I will accelerate into carefree adulthood now, I might have said
A body follows a mind to the edge, and then what?

•

I need these parameters around my speech
They push on me sensually, and yet I am always still listening for you
I'm too sensitive to receive criticism for longer than moments at a time
Mom says I'm getting too fat, and this is the Chinese way
She says look at your soft white hands
They're perfect she says you are perfect
May you never shove them down firmly into the farmed earth and pull
up a root vegetable
May you never flex them to delay atrophy
May you never sweat in an unbecoming way or see the past the way we
remember
In my past life I was a realist without the constitution for prose
Mom says I am so beautiful and overfed
Look at your smooth pale cuticles and oval nail beds
There is only one lifetime of praise in me, and I have not abandoned
nostalgia just yet

•

I said I would write for her in the new year and send the drafts home in
lieu of money
Unable to find the note that makes me sing, the text repeats my body
into another
Where is the song finally trained upon me?
Not among the neon signage of the street at night
This poem is not for you
I only promised to approach the opening and let my tenses slip
generously wide
This is where I come to be alone with words
I belly up to the sentence and live to construct this house for the vocal

    dead
Can you imagine:
We used to answer the phone to declare our unknowing
"Hello! I do not speak English!"
"Thank you!"
Who, is it you?
Why are you calling?
I echo out miles at a time but not to you[2]

Part Four

On Teaching

On Method

How to teach poetry? It seems good and right not to know; to keep trying different approaches. But to know that poetry is connected to life; to start there. In recent years, and among the upheavals in every aspect of how life is lived, I've taught an increasing number of poetry seminars and workshops centered around formally innovative poetry and the core elements of what we call documentary poetry, specifically the use of sourced texts, documents of institutional power, difficult to categorize forms, investigative and/or non-poetic texts, and avant-garde composition methods. In addition to offering students a wide range of powerful and politically lucid reading material, documentary writing is also particularly useful to the emerging writing for how it *foregrounds method and influence*, going as far as to imply that process is as important as content and subject. Cultivating an interest in process and the *how* of how poems get written is both challenging and essential. Documentary writing also implies, subversively, importantly, that *I* is not all there is. That the inner life is only a part. To find the rest, we turn to sourcing, scavenging, uncovering the conditions of production at work on each poem, and connect the work of the artist with the conditions of their time.

On Conditions

Documentary writing draws a clear line from writing as a technology to the culture-making memory devices of each age, be they print or increasingly digital, and offers emerging writers a resonant method of engagement with the world. As a genre that enthusiastically sources from emergent forms of connectivity and documentation, it offers students a generative methodology in alignment with their own *networked* lives. These texts help facilitate the kind of writing classrooms where macro questions (Why write? What is loneliness? What is power?) can be explored at the micro level, as students come to understand each technical choice as a proposed answer. Why did you *cut* that word out? Why did you *weave* those two transcripts together? Documentary writing doesn't allow for neutral actions nor neutral techniques.

Emerging writers are acutely aware that they write from conditions of unwanted documentation, surveillance, and the attention-fracturing speed of capitalism. Life, that thing that poetry is connected to, has never been more mediated by screens without guarantee of privacy or informed consent. Even as we repopulate physical spaces after Covid-19, the stakes of the issue remain. My students regularly express that they are concerned by the rise of the attention and outrage economies, the political violence of increased credentialization, collaboration and information sharing between their institutions and the police, tracking information, data, time stamps, avatars, platforms, and digital profiles. In my classes I've taken to calling all this broadly "unwanted documentations" and have invited the issues into the laboratory of the classroom, so that together, and in a controlled environment, students and I might (1) prove to ourselves that the stakes for engaging documentary praxis are literal, not merely conceptual or academic, and (2) collectively practice asserting our agency over the fraught ways we document and are documented by participating in the rich history of poets reappropriating documents of power and/or the state to aid in their production of creative work, and to speak back to power as self-appointed archivists of their time.

On Three Documentary Works

In a recent documentary poetry seminar, students self-designed a final creative work centered on whatever felt most urgent to them to explore, using a documentarian's ethos and toolbox. One particularly insightful final project of prose poems sourced the entirety of its language from the student's own written correspondence across emails, academic writing, and text messages, with the first half of the poems drawing exclusively from language written before Covid-19 was known to the world, and the second half drawn from language coming *after* that traumatic hinge, ultimately in search of what hopefulness unites the two halves of language rather than divides it. Is language its own premonition? How do the conditions of our moment in history manifest as disturbances in our most intimate language(s)?

Another writer overlaid original lyric poetry and elegy onto unwanted GPS maps of their own errands and trips during the pandemic, producing a secondary layer of rich emotional longing that is not legible in the sterility of data-driven documentation. A third project produced a long erasure poem sourced entirely from the (unwanted) transcript of the writer's Google Home to comment startlingly on surveillance, convenience, technological alienation, and consent.

A thread of deep feeling, curiosity, and care runs through these poetic experiments, buoyed by a pedagogy that takes seriously the issues that arise for students outside of the classroom. This is not to suggest that current events or personal experiences must always be the subject of their creative work, quite the opposite, as students discover their agency to connect literary techniques to the enormous ideas and frustrations (such as surveillance, or income inequality) that previously felt too omnipresent to tackle.

On Students

Students are not a monolith, not even college students, four-year college students, or private four-year college students studying writing (really). Across race, class, geography, disability, language, and other lines of experience, Covid-19 laid our pedagogical and accessibility shortcomings bare. Some of us adopted or evangelized existing "trauma-informed pedagogy," a slightly murky though right-headed set of responding actions implementable in any collective learning environment. Flexible deadlines, collective decision-making, circumstance-informed grading, and horizontal accountability are some of the most well known. But long before Covid-19 galvanized so many of us around one particular trauma, there has been good reason to tend in this direction. The specter of unemployment and other economic trauma has followed every graduating class of undergraduate and graduate students since at least 2008, compounded by the escalating crises of student loan debt and a stagnant minimum wage. My students are primarily working people, and many were "essential workers" in 2020 and 2021 despite what assumptions are often made about who is able to attend a New York City private university. Trauma-informed praxis does not *lower* standards or expectations for students in any way, rather it provides students with the circumstances and conditions to *rise* to the occasion (as we like to say), to meet those exact standards. It does not assume inability, in fact it assumes the opposite, with an added question: What do you need to best meet your ability today?

On American Literature

One of my central goals as an immigrant Asian American teacher of writing is to broaden my students' conception of what *American* literature means, and who is making it. My courses reflect a necessary belief that immigrant, diasporic, and multilingual literature *is* American literature, and must be centered. By encouraging students to abandon any preconceived ideas about the homogeneity of the field, they quickly notice the plethora of formal innovation that can be found in diverse writing traditions, and are less likely to succumb to the fallacy that writing centering "identity" and any number of American literary traditions—from the avant-garde, to the lyric, to the neo-formal—are segregated from one another. I strive to demonstrate to students that linguistic or formal experimentation in a poet's language is hardly arbitrary, rather, the manner and degree of innovation makes an argument to readers regarding language itself, and/or the poet's experience. For example, in a recent workshop, students discussed syntactical breakage as a representation of displacement and migration in Myung Mi Kim's *Under Flag* one week, laying the groundwork to understand reappropriated documentary language as an indictment of US military imperialism in Solmaz Sharif's *LOOK*, the next. Supplementary writing exercises utilized source texts with which students have their own "antagonistic" relationship (a plethora of contracts, applications for financial aid . . .) to provide pathways for harnessing these methodological and technical ideas, while still fresh, as generative forces for the construction of new work. In another recent course, students worked with two documentary erasure-poetry epics: Srikanth Reddy's *Voyager* and Chase Berggrun's *R E D*, and were invited to consider in an activity how their physical and psychic experiences of creating an erasure (cutting, lifting, removing) might complicate an authorial relationship to violence, trans-femme identity, the body, fragmentation, and history itself, especially across a book-length project with narrative goals. By deepening students' understanding of the inextricability of technique and intent, we may highlight each craft decision as a *proposal* of efficacy on the part of the author—a proposal that the student of writing may test, in order to better evaluate their original results. I've never found that students feel diminished by a documentary praxis, or by the suggestion that potentially the most interesting thing they can bring their attention to may very well be outside themselves. That they are *part of*, and may write as such.

On the First Day of Class

No matter how many times I do it, it still involves a variety of rituals, some to ward off fear, self-consciousness, others to attract confidence. There is a buzzing unsettledness, a gratitude, along with an uncertainty, an existential worry that something cosmic will go wrong.

Teaching is the only kind of public speaking that I like to do. When I have to give a speech, even in the context of teaching (say, giving remarks at a department gathering) I feel overwhelmed and sick, and I stumble over my words. When I give poetry readings, I stick to what's written on the page, though I might add a few remarks of greeting at the beginning. Reading poetry doesn't feel like public speaking to me, something closer to reading in public, or reading-to-myself-accidentally-in-public. I don't even have to look up if I don't want.

To say that the first meeting of a group of people is full of expectation, burden, assumption, and uncertainty is perhaps to say the obvious. But to continue to state what it's full of is to get somewhere interesting. How will I give or create agency, and how much will I keep for myself? What stands in the way of our shared or conflicting agency? Can I expect truth-telling? Should I? When will I project my assumptions and baggage and bias, and how will I catch myself? When will my students project their insecurities and fears (about agency? truth-telling?) onto me? Who will have authority and how can we pass and share it? How will we cultivate it for one another? Will our agendas align or conflict? How will we become audiences for one another in time?

These questions are good for the classroom, and good to repeat. My reluctance to be perceived, to stand-and-deliver in public on this very first day, reminds me that judgment and assumption are always with us, and the declaration of a classroom as a "safe space" or "judgment-free zone" (and other such popular terms) are just that, declarations. It takes active effort to perceive with slowness, care, accountability, without projection. It takes trying.

I'll welcome everybody, as I always do. I'll invite them to "get comfortable," take a few deep breaths, and maybe introduce yourself to the person sitting next to you today. They might be feeling frazzled, underslept, anxious, all of the above. I'll remind myself, too, that I should take a few deep breaths.

On Documents

I'll ask the group, "What kinds of documents are in your life?" and do you want them there? What documents and what forms are inextricably tied up with your selfhood, your agency? There will be some questions about what kinds of documents do I mean, to which I suppress the urge to say *exactly*! It doesn't seem helpful; it's an earnest question. I say any kind of document that comes to your mind is what I mean, I promise. Literal documents or things that feel like documents. Then I'll play some music and hope that it feels like a genuine, albeit short and timed, opportunity to think. It's difficult for me now to remember what exactly I expected students to come up with the first time I asked this question, or the second time, since by now I have so many memories of the surprising and varied things that they do say. But I know that I had once expected a limited, and literal, range of answers. Perhaps that students would offer "documents" relating to school, homework, part-time jobs. Maybe forms of identification that they are often asked for, some more than others. And I might have expected that it would be my role, wise and consciousness-expanding, to push them toward a wider more expansive definition of "document" and past literal types of "forms" that have coincided with their selfhood. Perhaps I imagined I would say something like what about . . . *social* forms? *Etiquette* as form? The police as carceral form?

The opportunity has never presented itself because my students are already thinking themselves there. They are living these thoughts as I imagine them needing me to lead them toward these thoughts.

They will name things like driver's licenses, passports, other forms of identification, birth certificates, marriage certificates. Others will say applications of all types, but specifically applications for part-time employment, federal student aid, scholarships to help pay for another semester at an expensive New York City university, reimbursement for medical procedures and mental health services, insurance claims. Someone might cite residency paperwork, someone else might say an exploitative job contract they are annually forced to resign in order to continue working to pay for school. Someone will definitely mention TikTok (it used to be Facebook), or Twitter, real-time documents that compete for one's attention 24/7. Most people will cite school and work as forms that rule their lives. Someone says family, someone else says homework and the patriarchy. I look forward to the sentimental answers, when someone ventures tentatively *is a photograph . . . a document?* It's of my girlfriend, I carry it around in my bag wherever I go. It's of my grandmother who passed away. Someone has a text message saved from years ago, the last communication from a lost friend. There are notes and letters from parents, song lyrics, rejection letters from internships and jobs and colleges, overdue bill notices, birth and death notices.

If I ask them to tell me about it, they'll confirm my feeling that their existing associations with "documentation" are overwhelmingly about bureaucracy, surveillance, and lack of agency. Though they want to change this. Documentation exists to slow down and impede the flow of resources toward those who need it most, to obfuscate the conditions of deprivation, marginalization, poverty, and need. Documents, and thus documentary forms, are necessarily withholding and institutional. They are agents of power, someone might offer. Mostly they enforce the status quo. Before long we're sharing our dreams with each other of self-determination, movement free from surveillance, wealth redistribution. The first day of class is off to a good start.

On Getting Outside Ourselves

At some point in the conversation, I do add that though we are talking about *everything*, we are also talking about *something* (a type of poetry) with conventions, parameters. These can also be contested, and hopefully we'll do exactly that this semester. Joseph Harrington has written helpfully and succinctly that "usually docupoetry designates poetry that 1) contains quotations from or reproductions of documents or statements not produced by the poet and 2) relates historical narratives, whether macro or micro, human or natural."[1] Is this like found poetry? Someone might ask. It is often a matter of finding, scavenging, I might answer. Of bringing in something outside yourself, to which there is nodding. Someone offers that the hardest thing to do in poetry is to write about something outside themselves. More nodding, vigorously. There is consensus that this is desirable, that writing outside ourselves supports thinking outside ourselves, moving with others, which is where solidarity begins.

We agree to pick up there, next time.

Notes

Reading Wang Wei in a Pandemic

1. Wang Wei, "9/9, Thinking of My Brothers East of the Mountains," trans. David Hinton, in *The Selected Poems of Wang Wei* (New York: New Directions, 2006), 1.

2. First published as part of "Meditations in a Crisis on Poems by Wang Wei, Enheduanna, and Ross Gay," *Jewish Currents*, May 15, 2020, https://jewishcurrents.org/provisions-4-here-in-a-foreign-place-my-thoughts-of-you-sharpen

Writing Home

1. Peter Beaumont, "Thirty Years On, the Tiananmen Square Image That Shocked the World," *The Guardian*, May 11, 2019, https://www.theguardian.com/world/2019/may/11/tank-man-photograph-tiananmen-square-30-years-jeff-widener

2. Peter Gizzi, "Extract from a Letter to Steve Farmer," in *American Poets in the 21st Century: The New Poetics*, ed. Claudia Rankine and Lisa Sewell (Middletown: Wesleyan University Press, 2007), 107–108.

3. Wendy Xu, *Phrasis* (New York: Fence Books, 2017).

4. Philip Metres, "From Reznikoff to Public Enemy," *Poetry Foundation*, 2007, https://www.poetryfoundation.org/articles/68969/from-reznikoff-to-public-enemy

5. Don Mee Choi, *Hardly War* (Seattle: Wave Books, 2016), 10.

6. Robin Coste Lewis, *Voyage of the Sable Venus and Other Poems* (New York: Alfred A. Knopf, 2015).

7. Srikanth Reddy, *Voyager* (Berkeley: University of California Press, 2011).

8. Layli Long Soldier, *Whereas* (Minneapolis: Graywolf Press, 2017).

9. Myung Mi Kim, *Under Flag* (Berkeley: Kelsey Street Press, 2008), originally published 1991.

10. Solmaz Sharif, *LOOK* (Minneapolis: Graywolf Press, 2016).

11. C. D. Wright, *One Big Self: An Investigation* (Port Townsend: Copper Canyon Press, 2007).

12. Liu Xiaobo, *June Fourth Elegies*, trans. Jeffrey Yang (Minneapolis: Graywolf Press, 2012).

13. Liu Xia, *Empty Chairs*, trans. Ming Di and Jennifer Stern (Minneapolis: Graywolf Press, 2015).

14. Bei Dao, *The August Sleepwalker*, trans. Bonnie S. McDougall (New York: New Directions Publishing, 1990).

15. Carolyn Forché, "Reading the Living Archives: The Witness of Literary Art," *Poetry Foundation*, May 2, 2011, https://www.poetryfoundation.org/poetrymagazine/articles/69680/reading-the-living-archives-the-witness-of-literary-art

Documentary Traces, Relatability, and the Limits of Witness

1. Ocean Vuong, "Amazon History of a Former Nail Salon Worker," in *Time Is a Mother* (New York: Penguin Press, 2022), 62–67.

2. Vuong, "Amazon History," 62.

3. Vuong, "Amazon History," 64.

4. Vuong, "Amazon History," 65–66.

5. Vuong, "Amazon History," 64–65.

6. Vuong, "Amazon History," 67.

7. Vuong, "Amazon History," 66.

8. Rebecca Mead, "The Scourge of Relatability," *New Yorker*, August 1, 2014, https://www.newyorker.com/culture/cultural-comment/scourge-relatability

9. Mead, "The Scourge of Relatability."

10. maple cocaine (@historyinflicks), "Conservatives: Lets round up Muslims and put them in camps, Liberals: HIRE MORE WOMEN GUARDS," Twitter, MARCH 9, 2017, 3:01 a.m., https://x.com/historyinflicks/status/839732795706593281?lang=en

11. Carolyn Forché, "Reading the Living Archives: The Witness of Literary Art," *Poetry Foundation*, May 2, 2011, https://www.poetryfoundation.org/poetrymagazine/articles/69680/reading-the-living-archives-the-witness-of-literary-art

12. Lyn Hejinian, "The Rejection of Closure," *Poetry Foundation*, October 13, 2009, https://www.poetryfoundation.org/articles/69401/the-rejection-of-closure

Notes from the Writing of an Unwritten Novel

1. "World Marks 30 Years Since Tiananmen Massacre as China Censors All Mention," *CNN World*, June 4, 2019, https://www.cnn.com/2019/06/03/asia/tiananmen-june-4-china-censorship-intl/index.html

2. "Tiananmen's Tank Man: The Image That China Forgot," *BBC World*, June 2, 2019, https://www.bbc.com/news/av/world-asia-48476879

3. *Diary of a Nurse*, directed by Jin Tao, performances by Danfeng Wang and Huada Tang (1957; Beijing).

Agoraphobe Logics

1. "The Ones Who Walk Away from Omelas," Wikipedia, last modified August 11, 2024, https://en.wikipedia.org/wiki/The_Ones_Who_Walk_Away_from_Omelas

2. "Liu Xia: Widow of Nobel Laureate Arrives in Berlin After Release from China," *The Guardian*, July 10, 2018, https://www.theguardian.com/world/2018/jul/10/liu-xia-nobel-laureates-widow-allowed-to-leave-china-for-europe

3. David Naimon, "Between the Covers: Solmaz Sharif Interview," *Tin House*, 2022, https://tinhouse.com/transcript/between-the-covers-solmaz-sharif-interview/

4. Paul Carter, *Repressed Spaces: The Poetics of Agoraphobia* (London: Reaktion Books, 2004).

5. Liu Xia, *Empty Chairs*, trans. Ming Di and Jennifer Stern (Minneapolis: Graywolf Press, 2015).

6. Xia, "Scheme," in *Empty Chairs*, 13.

7. Xia, "Scheme," 13.

8. Xia, "Scheme," 13.

9. Xia, "Misplaced," in *Empty Chairs*, 55.

10. Xia, "Misplaced," 55.

11. Xia, "It's Only Waking Up," in *Empty Chairs*, 67.

12. Xia, "It's Only Waking Up," 67.

13. Xia, "Untitled," in *Empty Chairs*, 97.

14. Xia, "Misplaced," 55.

Monologue on Intention

1. I revisited, on the occasion of a reading for the Double Take Reading Series in November 2017 (New York), my history with the word "intention" (all tenses of the word) as documented in email. An email travelogue in

reverse of sorts, fittingly unintentional. I was interested in that muckiest, most disordered, most banal, most daily, most prodigious, and most neglected archive, the inbox, and what it had stored of my best or worst intentions from 2014 to 2017, my earliest days in New York City.

Disappear Yourself

1. Adam Johnson and Othman Ali, "Coverage of Gaza War in the New York Times and Other Major Newspapers heavily Favorited Israel, Analysis Shows," *The Intercept*, January 9, 2024, https://theintercept.com/2024/01/09/newspapers-israel-palestine-bias-new-york-times

2. Henri Michaux, *Miserable Miracle*, trans. Louise Varese (New York: New York Review Books, 2002).

3. Reinhard Kuhn, "The Hermeneutics of Silence: Michaux and Mescaline," *Yale French Studies*, no. 50 (1974): 131.

4. Michaux, *Miserable Miracle*, 16.

5. Michaux, *Miserable Miracle*, 42–59.

6. Akane Kawakami, "Illegible Writing: Michaux, Masson, and Dotremont," *Modern Language Review* 106, no. 2 (2011): 388–406, https://doi.org/10.5699/modelangrevi.106.2.0388

7. Andrew Joron, "Thousand Times Broken: Gilian Conoley on the Works of Henri Michaux," *Poetry Foundation*, November 18, 2014, https://www.poetryfoundation.org/blog/open-door/71648/thousand-times-broken-gillian-conoley-on-the-works-of-henri-michaux

8. Chase Berggrun, *R E D* (New York: Birds LLC, 2016).

9. Berggrun, *R E D*, 45.

10. Ruby Brunton, "The Feminine and the Bloodthirsty: Chase Berggrun Interviewed," *Bomb Magazine*, August 6, 2018, https://bombmagazine.org/articles/2018/08/06/chase-berggrun/

11. Berggrun, *R E D*, 25.

12. Berggrun, *R E D*, 35.

13. Berggrun, *R E D*, 32.

14. Berggrun, *R E D*, 45.

15. Berggrun, *R E D*, 8.

16. Berggrun, *R E D*, 34.

Things to Do with Form

1. Bhanu Kapil, *How to Wash a Heart* (Liverpool: Liverpool University Press, 2020).

2. Ocean Vuong, "Amazon History of a Former Nail Salon Worker," in *Time Is a Mother* (New York: Penguin Press, 2022), 62–67.

3. Sarah Jean Alexander, "Please Eat," *Cargo Collective*, accessed August 16, 2017, http://cargocollective.com/please-eat, site inactive 2024.

4. Amber Atiya, "New York State Office of Temporary and Disability Food Stamps SSI Benefits Application," *Literary Hub*, June 24, 2015, https://bookmarks.reviews/new-york-state-office-of-temporary-and-disability-assistance-ssifood-stamp-benefits-application/

5. Robin Coste Lewis, *Voyage of the Sable Venus and Other Poems* (New York: Knopf, 2015).

6. M. NourbeSe Philip, *Zong!* (Middletown: Wesleyan University Press, 2011).

7. Henri Michaux, *Miserable Miracle*, trans. Louise Varese (New York: New York Review Books, 2002).

8. Philip Metres, *Sand Opera* (Farmington: Alice James Books, 2015).

9. Sean Bonney, *Baudelaire in English* (Guildford: Veer Books, 2008).

10. Stéphane Mallarmé, *The Book*, trans. Sylvia Gorelick (Cambridge: Exact Change Books, 2018).

11. Diana Khoi Nguyen, *Ghost Of* (Richmond: Omnidawn, 2018).

12. giovanni singleton, *American Letters: Works on Paper* (Marfa: Canarium Books, 2016).

13. Nicole Sealey, *The Ferguson Report: An Erasure* (New York: Knopf, 2023).

14. Layli Long Soldier, *Whereas* (Minneapolis: Graywolf Press, 2017).

15. Mai Der Vang, *Yellow Rain* (Minneapolis: Graywolf Press, 2021).

16. Kazim Ali, "The 'Tradition' of the Fragment," *Poetry Foundation*, 2019, https://www.poetryfoundation.org/harriet-books/2019/04/the-tradition-of-the-fragment

17. Bertolt Brecht, *War Primer* (Brooklyn: Verso Books, 2017).

18. Don Mee Choi, *Hardly War* (Seattle: Wave Books, 2016).

Ghost(s) Of

1. Diana Khoi Nguyen, *Ghost Of* (Richmond: Omnidawn, 2018).

2. Diana Khoi Nguyen, "The Exodus," in *Ghost Of*, 32–34.

3. Diana Khoi Nguyen, "Triptych," in *Ghost Of*, 19–21.

4. Kazim Ali, "The 'Tradition' of the Fragment," *Poetry Foundation*, April 16, 2019, https://www.poetryfoundation.org/featured-blogger/81665/the-tradition-of-the-fragment

5. Diana Khoi Nguyen, "Gyotaku," in *Ghost Of*, 46–47.

6. Khoi Nguyen, "Gyotaku," 26–27.

7. Khoi Nguyen, "Gyotaku," 52–53.

8. Khoi Nguyen, "Gyotaku," 27.
9. Khoi Nguyen, "Gyotaku," 64–65.
10. Anne Carson, introduction to *If Not, Winter: Fragments of Sappho*, trans. Anne Carson (New York: Vintage, 2003), xi.
11. Qiu Zhijie, *Writing the Orchid Pavilion Preface One Thousand Times*, 1990–1995, M+Sigg Collection Hong Kong, https://www.metmuseum.org/art/collection/search/77606
12. Mahmoud Darwish, *In the Presence of Absence*, trans. Sinan Antoon (Brooklyn: Archipelago Books, 2011), 72.
13. Othman Moqbel, "Across the Western World Public Opinion on Palestine Is Finally Shifting," *Aljazeera*, April 26, 2024, https://www.aljazeera.com/opinions/2024/4/26/across-the-western-world-public-opinion-on-palestine-is-finally-shifting

giovanni singleton's American Forms (Black Sisyphus; Don't Shoot)

1. giovanni singleton, "Black Sisyphus–Take the High Road (a quadriptych: presently) in *American Letters: Works on Paper* (Marfa: Canarium Books, 2016), 51–55.
2. singleton, "illustrated equation no. 1," in *American Letters*, 42–44.
3. singleton, "illustrated equation," 41.
4. Joyelle McSweeney, "The Rose of Sound," *Tendon Magazine*, 2020.
5. singleton, "illustrated equation," 44.
6. singleton, "illustrated equation," 44.

Three Transformations

1. Rachel Stone, "The Trump-Era Boom in Erasure Poetry," *New Republic*, October 23, 2017, https://newrepublic.com/article/145396/trump-era-boom-erasure-poetry
2. Layli Long Soldier, *Whereas* (Minneapolis: Graywolf Press, 2017).
3. Long Soldier, *Whereas*, 57.
4. Resolution of Apology to Native Peoples of the United States, S.J. Res. 14, 111th Cong. (2008).
5. Resolution (2).
6. Resolution (5).
7. Layli Long Soldier, "Resolution (1)," in *Whereas*, 89.
8. Layli Long Soldier, "Resolution (2)," in *Whereas*, 90.
9. Long Soldier, "Resolution (2)," 90, lines 1–5.
10. Long Soldier, "Resolution (2)," 90, lines 4–9.
11. Layli Long Soldier, "Ȟe Sápa," in *Whereas*, 8.
12. Layli Long Soldier, "Resolution (3)," in *Whereas*, 91.

13. Long Soldier, "Resolution (3)," 91n.

14. Amber Atiya, "New York State Office of Temporary and Disability Food Stamps SSI Benefits Application," *Literary Hub*, June 24, 2015, https://bookmarks.reviews/new-york-state-office-of-temporary-and-disability-assistance-ssifood-stamp-benefits-application/

15. Atiya, "New York State," lines 1–11.

16. The Friend, introduction to "New York State Office of Temporary and Disability Food Stamps SSI Benefits Application," *Literary Hub*, June 24, 2015, https://bookmarks.reviews/new-york-state-office-of-temporary-and-disability-assistance-ssifood-stamp-benefits-application/

17. Atiya, "New York State," lines 46–47.

18. Atiya, "New York State," line 25.

19. Atiya, "New York State," lines 24, 26–29.

20. Atiya, "New York State," lines 35–37, 40–43.

21. Sarah Jean Alexander, "Please Eat," *Cargo Collective*, accessed August 16, 2017, http://cargocollective.com/please-eat, site inactive 2024.

22. Alexander, "Please Eat," lines 1–33.

23. Alexander, "Please Eat," line 12.

24. Alexander, "Please Eat," lines 113, 213.

25. Alexander, "Please Eat," lines 94, 146, 236, 289, 298.

26. Alexander, "Please Eat," lines 123–146.

27. Alexander, "Please Eat," lines 171, 257.

28. Alexander, "Please Eat," lines 127, 74, 245.

29. Alexander, "Please Eat," line 329.

The Destruction of the Earth Is the Destruction of All Childhoods

1. "History of Degrowth," Degrowth.info, accessed August 10, 2024, https://degrowth.info/en/history

2. Inger Christensen, *Alphabet*, trans. Susanna Nied (New York: New Directions, 2001).

3. Hannah Cooper-Smithson, "Toward a Pandemic Poetics: Contamination, Infiltration, and Dispersal in Inger Christensen's Alphabet," *Configurations* 29, no. 4 (2021): 405–416, https://dx.doi.org/10.1353/con.2021.0029

4. Christensen, *Alphabet*, 11–14.

5. Cooper-Smithson, "Toward a Pandemic Poetics," 408.

6. Christensen, *Alphabet*, 14, line 2.

7. Christensen, *Alphabet*, 16, lines 7–9.

8. Christensen, *Alphabet*, 24–25.

9. Sharon Lerner, "How 3M Discovered, Then Concealed, the Dangers of Forever Chemicals," *New Yorker*, May 20, 2024, https://www.newyorker.com/magazine/2024/05/27/3m-forever-chemicals-pfas-pfos-toxic

10. Chris Jordan, *Midway, Message from the Gyre*, 2009–2013, photo series, accessed August 10, 2023, https://www.chrisjordan.com/Midway/4/thumbs-caption

11. Anna Turns, "The Photo That Made the Plastics Crisis Personal," *BBC*, June 2, 2023, https://www.bbc.com/future/article/20230531-the-photo-that-changed-the-worlds-response-to-the-plastics-crisis

12. Lerner, "How 3M Discovered."

13. Gertrude Stein, "Portraits and Repetitions," in *Gertrude Stein: Writings, 1932–1946*, ed. Catharine R. Stimpson and Harriet Chessman (New York: Library of America, 1998), 292, 288.

14. Christensen, *Alphabet*, 31, lines 20–21.

15. Quoted in Dorothee Sölle, *Against the Wind: Memoir of a Radical Christian* (Minneapolis: Fortress, 1999), 139.

16. Christensen, *Alphabet*, 30, lines 2–11.

17. Diane Di Prima, "Revolutionary Letter #15," in *Revolutionary Letters* (San Francisco: Last Gasp, 2007), 27, lines 1–5.

18. Christensen, *Alphabet*, 60–61, lines 25–30, 1–10.

19. Christensen, *Alphabet*, 76–77, lines 19–22, 1–3.

What Is the Present For?

1. First published as "Short Conversations with Poets: Wendy Xu by Jesse Nathan," *McSweeney's*, March 9, 2022, https://www.mcsweeneys.net/articles/wendy-xu

Notes for a Canceled Short Lecture on Reversible and Coded Form(s)

1. Bei Dao, "Black Map," trans. Eliot Weinberger, in *The Rose of Time: New and Selected Poems* (New York: New Directions, 2010), 253, line 9.

2. Bei Dao, "Notes from the City of the Sun," trans. Bonnie S. McDougall, in *The Rose of Time*, 3.

3. Bei Dao, "Notes," lines 26–27.

4. Bei Dao, "Notes," lines 7–19.

5. Bei Dao, "Notes," lines 8–10.

6. Bei Dao, "Notes," lines 41–42.

7. Bei Dao, "Notes from the City of the Sun," trans. Bonnie S. McDougall, in *Notes from the City of the Sun: Poems* (Ithaca: Cornell University East Asia Papers, 1983).

8. Bei Dao, "Notes," trans. McDougall, lines 34–37.

9. Bei Dao, "Notes," trans. McDougall, line 19.

10. Refrain, *Su Hui's Xuanjitu*, August 18, 2015, accessed July 2024, https://en.wikipedia.org/wiki/Star_Gauge#/media/File:Xuanjitu.png

11. Michèle Métail, “Su Hui: The Map of the Armillary Sphere,” in *Wild Geese Returning: Chinese Reversible Poems*, trans. Jody Gladding (Hong Kong: Chinese University of Hong Kong Press, 2011), 9–13.

12. Emily Lee Luan, 回 / *Return* (New York: Nightboat Books, 2023).

13. Wendy Xu, “Interview: Emily Lee Luan,” *BOMB*, October 19, 2023, https://bombmagazine.org/articles/2023/10/19/emily-lee-luan/

14. Emily Lee Luan, “She’s the Only One Who Hears Me Sing,” 回 / *Return*, 29.

15. Emily Lee Luan, “Notes on Reversing,” *futurefeed*, 2023, https://future-feed.net/notes-on-reversing

16. Luan, “She’s the Only One,” 29, lines 1–8.

17. Luan, “Notes on Reversing.”

18. This sentiment or similar precedes Internal Family Systems, and echoes the powerful closing line of June Jordan’s 1978 poem decrying apartheid, “Poem for South African Women,” which reads, “we are the ones we’ve been waiting for.”

Wendy Xu and Emily Lee Luan on Return, Form, and Longing

1. Emily Lu Gao, “An Interview with Emily Lee Luan on Her Debut, 回 / *Return*,” *Nightboat Books Blog*, April 25, 2023, https://nightboat.org/flip-it-and-reverse-it-interview-with-emily-luan-on-her-debut-%E5%9B%9E-return/

2. A shortened version of this conversation first published as “Interview: Emily Lee Luan,” *BOMB*, October 19, 2023, https://bombmagazine.org/articles/2023/10/19/emily-lee-luan/

What I Don’t Know About ’89

1. Roger Ebert, “The Gospel According to St. Matthew,” RoberEbert.com, March 14, 2004, https://www.rogerebert.com/reviews/great-movie-gospel-according-to-st-matthew-1964

2. Deping Xu, “Winter Day,” 2023.

3. Deping Xu, “Seeking and Visiting Plum Blossoms in the Snow,” 2024.

Notes for an Opening (2015–2020)

1. Não Collective, “The Poetry and Brief Life of a Foxconn Worker: Xu Lizhi (1990–2014),” Libcom, October 29, 2014, https://libcom.org/article/poetry-and-brief-life-foxconn-worker-xu-lizhi-1990-2014

2. Parts of this long project of memoir, poetics, resentment, and lyrical

discontent were excerpted and published variously in journals and as "Notes for an Opening" in *The Past* (2021), and "A Sound Not Unlike a Bell" (Triple Canopy, 2018). This is the complete version, spanning the years 2015–2020.

On Teaching

1. Joseph Harrington, "Docupoetry and Archive Desire," *Jacket2*, October 27, 2011, https://jacket2.org/article/docupoetry-and-archive-desire